£1.99
16/11

Hillie Marshall's
Guide To
Successful
Relationships

Foreword by
Nicholas Parsons

SUMMERSDALE

Summersdale Publishers
46 West Street
Chichester
West Sussex
PO19 1RP
United Kingdom

A CIP catalogue record for this book is available from the British Library.

ISBN 1 873475 33 0

Printed and bound in Great Britain
by Selwood Printing Ltd., Burgess Hill.

To Alan
- my main source of inspiration for this book.

To Anne and Kelly for all their sympathy and support.

To Nicola and Jamie, my children,
for just being themselves and being there for me.

To Stewart and Alastair for placing their trust in me.

To my mother without whom this book would never
have been written!

Contents

Foreword

by Nicholas Parsons

Relationships govern everything in our lives. They affect us all in so many different ways, both in our work and at home. In order to exist we are continually creating and forging relationships, and according to how successful we are, depends to a great extent on the success we achieve in our work and harmony in our personal lives.

There is a character in Bernard Shaw's play, *Man and Superman*, who says, 'Do not do unto others as you would they should do unto you. Their tastes may not be the same'. This is a witty way of commenting on the difficulty most people experience in relating to one another. It is probably because relationships can never be considered in isolation from personality. The ones we make in developing friendship, romance or just a sexual encounter, are all related to personality. We respond to another human being according to our emotional make-up, and the predominate attraction to which we respond, may be physical, cerebral, or some indefinable quality or character trait that ignites a spark within us. It can on occasions be only one factor, and when that happens we are usually fully aware of what it is, but on the whole the attraction is based on a number of disparate factors, that only a deep understanding of our unconscious would probably reveal. This book, however, is not concerned with an analysis of unconscious motives. It is looking at the situation from the outside. It is not attempting a deep psychiatric interpretation of what attracts one person to another. It is endeavouring to be a simple and helpful guide for those who wish to understand what prompts or motivates them in the various relationships they make throughout their lives. This awareness can be valuable in making good judgements, fair assessments, and hopefully avoid unfortunate liaisons that may lead to distress, unhappiness or emotional turmoil.

In our adult life we are constantly being required to relate to somebody, even in the most mundane situations as we go about our daily business, be it in a shop, a bank or on the telephone. In all situations life becomes easier when a rapport can be made with the person with whom we are speaking. The major relationships that occur in our lives are those where physical attraction is involved, which may develop into something intense or significant, and perhaps even lasting. Other major relationships can be equally important on occasions, such as those created in your place of work with your immediate colleagues, or with those above employing you, or with those for whom you have responsibility and are required to organise. Depending on how successful you are, will affect the harmony that exists in your working conditions, and often the possibilities of your advancement. Some people find this process of communicating with their fellow beings easy, others difficult. It depends on your emotional make-up. Some may have a natural gift for communicating, but what they are doing basically is accepting that we are all different, and it is instinctive for them to relate to others by simply making allowances for that difference in temperament that exists in us all. If you are not a naturally intuitive person, it is necessary to make that conscious effort if success in relationships is important. There are some naturally cussed individuals who are not interested in getting along with people, in making any good relationship. Some even seem to revel, through arrogance or pride, in making bad relationships. Perhaps it gives them some perverse joy, or they are naturally unhappy people. This book should hopefully help them, if they are prepared to change. It is, however, written principally for those with a positive attitude to living, who wish to improve their understanding of themselves and others, and move forward in all aspects of their life.

As an Actor, one is very aware of relationships. We are calling on our emotions all the time in our work to express thoughts, feelings, ideas. Working on a stage probably requires more emotional energy than any other job, and to be successful it is necessary to communicate this highly charged energy to others. Some actors are naturally instinctive, and can tap into their nervous and emotional energy with incredible ease. Perhaps it is for this reason, some do not have the same success in making a lasting relationship on a personal basis. So much of their response is of a more transient nature, communicating rapidly and making a relationship with an audience, which finishes once the curtain falls or the audience goes home. Actors are also very privileged in that they experience more instant communication with people when working to an audience some of which can be difficult as well as easy, but if they are analytical can give them a great deal of insight into human nature.

I first met Hillie in a theatrical situation. She had engaged me to perform in one of the Old Tyme Music Hall shows she presents and appears in herself, through her production company, Edwardians Unlimited. On a personal level a friendship rapidly developed. There was that empathy that often occurs in show business, where we are all struggling for the same ends and our emotions are near the surface. I soon realised what a sensitive and caring person she was, and have been impressed with how she has developed her awareness and understanding of others over a period of many years. Drawing undoubtedly on her work as a performer, discovering those qualities that are required to make a relationship with an audience, and later coming to terms with the emotional stress in her own life, and applying all this, she has discovered what is required to make successful personal relationships. She has carried her abilities in this area and her natural skill in communicating with people into helping others to achieve happy and successful relationships through her Dinner Dates organisation, bringing together single people anxious to meet someone with similar interests, and hoping to form a friendship or a more intimate liaison, and leading perhaps to something permanent. As her business has grown she has become a spontaneous friend to thousands, a natural counsellor to many, and through the success of this work evolved into writing as an Agony Aunt in a dating magazine, and now dispensing advice on the Internet.

The first relationship anyone makes in life is with their Mother, and depending on how good that bonding is at a tender age, will often depend how secure that person feels as they grow up, and it can affect their ability to develop into a stable mature human being and make good relationships. This may be a fairly simplistic statement, since there are so many factors involved in anyone's development, and we are all naturally conditioned by the temperament with which we have been born and the environment in which we grow up. Also conditioning throughout our lives can be affected by the many relationships we are forever making, first with immediate family, then at school, then perhaps at university, then in the work-place; and at some time during this later period, a relationship with someone to whom we are attracted. This is to many the challenging and difficult relationship, as our emotions are involved in quite a different and unsettling way. You would imagine with all the practice over many years with so many different people and in so many different circumstances, it would be easy. To some it may, but to many it can be difficult, even disturbing, because so many conflicting emotions are involved. It can be fun and exciting, and indeed it should be, but not all of us in the stressful world in which most of us live today seem able to encompass it in that delightfully straightforward way we dreamed about when young. When this does happen and the responses between two individuals are entirely mutual, how fortunate we are. Whatever first attracts two people together, however, the relationship that is formed has to be worked on. It can never be taken for granted, especially when the initial attraction was not all embracing. There are so many emotional factors involved, and as we grow older many of us develop or mature in different ways. Bernard Shaw with that profound logic he so often displayed, has a character, again from his play, *Man and Superman*, say, 'The reasonable man adapts himself to the world; the unreasonable one persists in trying to adapt the world to himself. Therefore all progress depends on the unreasonable man'. Reasonable or unreasonable we all wish to make progress, and often the way to achieve this is to adapt, particularly to each other. If you have not discovered the secret or the way ahead, this book has been devised to help. Please read on.

Introduction

Life is one constant battle to develop, maintain and repair relationships. They are the primary obsession for most people: problems with relationships consume most of our waking hours, solutions are hard enough to find, and we waste valuable time on them, instead of getting on with the general job of living.

Relationships, like a car, need regular servicing and repairs. But, unlike a car, there is no manual to tell you how to do it. If you attempt to repair a car without any idea which part is which, you are likely to damage it even more, and most of us will be aware of this fact. But we all try to repair damaged relationships without knowing what we are doing. This book aims to be the manual of relationships. It will help guide people in forming new relationships of all kinds. It will give advice to those already in a relationship that will help to make the relationship work, and also give vital tips on restoring and repairing problems in any kinds of relationships.

This book is not necessarily meant to be read from cover to cover like a novel. Although the book develops from its opening chapter *What are relationships?* through to friendships, attracting someone, talking, dating, keeping the relationship going, marriage, the seven year itch, and finally gives advice on what to do if you have to start all over again, it can be used as a guide book.

If for example you are having problems in making your relationship a success, then refer to *Chapter 6* to start with and move on from there. If you are trying to cope with the break up of a relationship, start at *Chapter 9* and then move to the beginning of the book. This book attempts to help everyone, whatever their needs may be, in attempting to achieve and maintain a successful relationship.

Chapter 1

What are relationships?

Definition
Relationships are the loose structure that bind mankind together. The myriad of interconnections between people consist of love, loyalty, respect, fear and many other emotional reasons why people care about each other. People feel isolated from those around them if they are not bound in some way by a relationship, no matter how loose.

Our first relationships
When we begin life as a baby we are fairly cocooned, and we are dependent primarily on the love and care of our mother. We learn to trust and communicate our needs with her, and then with our father and any other carers looking after us. As a toddler we build relationships with just a few friends to begin with, and as we grow older and start going to school we get to know more people.

Our first relationships with parents, other children, people in authority, and animals, are vitally important in preparing us for the complex adult world.

We begin to recognise the various types of people around us and how to deal with them. We learn to treat the bully in the playground with care, keeping our distance and learning how to cope with fear of others. We find there are those around us with whom we can relax and have fun. We learn self preservation and how to behave towards others. We soon find out that if we hit another child in the playground they will hit us back, and this elementary learning forms a basis for the way in which we lead our adult lives.

We endeavour to learn how to control our feelings, such as disappointment or anger. We find out that if we throw tantrums when things go wrong for us, and then blame and abuse others, people will not like us, we will lose our friends and probably be punished by those in authority. We learn that if we lie, are deceitful or dishonest, we will be punished. If we are constantly crying and feeling sorry for ourselves, if we are totally self absorbed and show no interest in other people's emotions and activities, our friends will get bored and abandon us. We build up relationships with our teachers and hopefully learn to respect their knowledge and accept their discipline. We spend many years in a safe environment learning the boundaries of what we can or cannot do in our relationships with others.

We start learning to spot different types of characters in the people we meet and to adjust our own character accordingly in our dealings with them. Some friends always make us laugh and we tend to approach them in a jovial manner, and it is natural to enjoy the company of those with a sunny disposition. In the same way, we may turn on the television to see our favourite comedian, and find ourselves smiling before even they have said anything. If this is the effect that another can have over us, we should learn to develop our own personality so that our friends are pleased to see us and smile. We communicate in different ways to different age groups. For example we would talk differently to our parents than we would to our friends - we probably wouldn't swear in front of our parents or tell them our most intimate secrets in the same way that we would with close friends of similar age.

At home we may have brothers or sisters that we have to learn to get on with in close proximity, and we may even share a bedroom with them - we learn to be considerate and allow them their space, otherwise they will make life uncomfortable for us. We learn to tolerate their annoying habits and untidiness, and also to cope with sibling rivalry and jealousy. If we have a younger brother or sister we learn responsibility towards them and an ability to look after someone else. When a member of the household is sick we learn sympathy and how to care for them.

Our relationship with our grandparents is an important one, in that we learn care and tolerance toward older people. We may also, if they are elderly, experience the grief of death, how to cope with it and how to comfort our parents and those close to us.

Unfortunately many childhood experiences can be detrimental in our development toward good adult relationships. For some children, especially those who are ultra sensitive or too young, boarding school can have an adverse effect. Some children locked away at a early age can become introverted and build up such emotional barriers that in later years they may find it impossible to open up to people and express their feelings.

Some children become so over competitive that they constantly have to achieve the best marks in class or be the best at sports and would see it as a weakness in themselves if they failed. In later life they may develop an inability to question themselves if things go wrong in a relationship, for fear of discovery that the problem might lie within them.

If a child comes from a home where the parents are unhappily married he/she may develop a fear of commitment to a relationship. They will form an idealistic idea of a relationship, and build up a mental image of their perfect partner that is so totally unachievable that they will never be able to commit themselves to anybody. They are committed to non commitment!

A child from an unhappy home, and who might also have been mentally abused, may be so conditioned to living in a stressful unhappy atmosphere that in later years they have to create that same strife within their relationships, as it is the norm for them. They make themselves become a victim, as they have an inability to cope with a happy relationship. Some children do not succeed at doing anything very well at school, and therefore have low expectations of their own worth. Later in life this can cause problems if they find themselves in a successful relationship, as they may unwittingly sabotage it, because they only have experience of failure.

Sometimes boys who have been brought up by an overpowering and domineering mother will develop into men who have an inner hatred for women, and feel a need to abuse them in some way.

If a boy is brought up in a household where his father treats his mother with disrespect and abuse, again he may well grow into a man who treats women in the same way, believing it to be the norm.

In childhood, if a girl sees her mother receiving love, she will know how to receive it; if she sees her mother being treated badly by men she will probably expect all men to behave that way, and will therefore not have learnt how to receive love.

If a child is sexually abused they will find it almost impossible, without professional help, to have a satisfactory relationship with a partner. They will also feel unworthy and rejected.

Many children will grow into adults who try to recreate their mother or father in the person they have a relationship with. I have met women who go from one failed relationship to another as they choose men who are identical to their father, and who made their lives such a misery in their childhood.

As a child we are very often given a pet, such as a dog. The relationship with a dog is a simple one, for they give love unconditionally, no matter what the looks or character of the owner may be. On the other hand, human love, outside of the immediate family, generally has to be earned. A dog does not have subtle emotions, they are either extremely happy, extremely sad or bored, and they make no effort to hide these feelings. We learn that our emotions can effect our pet - if we are happy they are happy, if we are sad they are too - just as our emotions affect other human beings. We learn to have good relations with our pets, and find out that if we are kind to a dog it will wag its tail, and if we are unkind it will feel hurt, insecure and unhappy. The same is true with humans, and we have to be kind and good to get a human tail wagging! Human emotional responses are harder to notice: the *tail* is invisible and we have to learn to pick up more subtle signs of how another person is feeling.

Some adults find relationships with other humans very difficult or even undesirable, and prefer the less complicated type of relationship that comes from owning a pet. Some women find that owning a dog is good preparation for eventually having a baby of their own. If she feels she is not yet ready to have a baby, she may start getting broody to have a dog instead. As she learns to look after it and accept responsibility for its total dependence on her, she grows up within herself, and one day, completely out of the blue, she will find herself wanting to have a baby!

Differences between men and women in looking for a relationship of various kinds.
To simplify this complex subject, it could be argued that men tend to judge women from a physical perspective and women tend to judge men from an emotional one. By this I mean that a man wants a woman to look good, be a good lover, and be the envy of all his friends. A woman wants a man who listens to her and says the right things, consoles her when she is unhappy, and makes her laugh.

Women
Women need the friendship and companionship of other women to keep them sane! They look for someone in whom they can trust, share confidences and discuss their problems - especially those concerning men. They will look for friends who share their own female interests and which a man might not be able to relate to.

A woman may also look for platonic friendships with men with whom they can have some fun and discuss issues from a man's point of view. It is also pleasant to have a male friend she can call upon to escort her to functions without the worry of him misconstruing her intentions.

In a relationship with a partner women are looking for friendship, caring, understanding, respect, trust, devotion, validation, reassurance, support, security, and a sense of humour. A woman also needs to feel loved and cherished to be able to blossom in a relationship. Communication is of primary importance, and talking and relating to her partner brings tremendous fulfilment. A woman also wants a listener, not someone who tells her what to do.

An older woman may well have the conflict of looking for the younger man of her dreams with plenty of romance, at the same time looking for the security and lifestyle of the more mature man.

A woman's sense of self worth is defined through her feelings and the quality of her relationships.

Men
A man will look for the companionship of other men with whom he can share the same pursuits, such as sport or going to the pub for a drink. Men often need other men to talk to in a more *vulgar* way than they would to a woman. They need to discuss their business affairs, and also their problems with women with a male friend.

Men also seek platonic relationships with women with whom they can discuss their problems and various issues, and listen to a woman's point of view without emotional feelings getting in the way.

In a relationship with a partner men are looking for trust, acceptance, appreciation, admiration, approval, encouragement and support, friendship, love, a sense of humour, and total loyalty. A man needs to feel needed and will feel motivated and empowered when he is. A man also needs a woman who is prepared to give him his space and not be over possessive. A man likes to be in control and, although he will admire strength in a woman, does not want to be controlled in a relationship. A man will seek a woman who is not over emotional and who will not put emotional pressure on him. A man wants a woman who can be independent, and give him his independence as well as nurturing and looking after him. A man looks for his partner to be a *whore* in the bedroom, a cook in the kitchen, and a *lady* in public. Try listening to the song *Behind Closed Doors* performed by Charlie Rich.

An older man may well have the conflict of wanting a bimbo on his arm, to make him feel young and gain the envy of his peers, at the same time wanting to be looked after by a mother image.

Whatever sex you are, we are all looking to feel comfortable, with a sense of belonging, in a relationship. Also remember that if you are not ready to compromise your ideals you will never form a lasting relationship, as there is no such thing as the perfect person. There are possibly thousands of people out there who would be perfect for us, it is just a matter of recognising them when you meet them. Sometimes there is someone who is just right for us *under our nose* but we are too blind to see it! Many years ago people used to live in the same village and never leave it all their lives. They still managed to meet someone, fall in love and get happily married. Maybe nowadays we are just spoilt for choice. Recognise what your relationship really is, and if it is enjoyable don't start thinking how different it should be to make it perfect. Provided any problems you may have are not insurmountable, talk about them, compromise and be satisfied - you'll be amazed how much happier you will feel.

Chapter 2

Friendship

Why we need friends

Humans are social animals who don't like to exist alone, and most of us need friends because we would feel lonely without any. Some people, such as a hermit or a recluse, do not find loneliness a problem, but others need to have contact with the outside world through having friends. Basically most of us like to feel needed by someone.

It is good to have friends to share experiences with, and a shared experience is twice as good as having one on your own. It is more fun to go, for example, to the theatre, cinema or football match with a friend than by yourself. It is good to be able to talk about what has been happening in your life and listen to their bits of news; how dull life would be without the opportunity to have a good gossip with a friend. Half the fun of going on holiday is taking snapshots and videos that you can *bore* your friends with on your return. Many competitive sports like tennis or squash would be impossible to participate in without a friend to play with.

What is a friend?

A friend is someone you know who is more than an acquaintance. For example someone with whom you work and share platitudes and pleasantries could be an acquaintance, however, if you then begin to share confidences with them and meet them outside working hours to do things together, they become a friend. A friend is someone you can trust; someone you know well and, to whom you can impart personal information that you would not dream of telling an acquaintance.

Why people find themselves without friends

People find themselves without friends for all kinds of reasons. Sometimes it is geographic movement in that they are relocated in their job to a new area and don't know anyone. Other reasons could be the death of their friend; an inability to make friends because of excessive shyness; someone who has an innate distrust of strangers and is afraid of making an approach to, or being approached by a potential friend; or merely a complete lack of effort in even trying to make friends.

Some people have no friends because they are unpopular and lack sufficient objectivity to look into themselves to see what the problem could be. A classic example of this is *Mr Bean* - just watch the videos. Here is someone who has no sense of style, taste, humour, human understanding, interests or ambition. He shares the same desires for human companionship as anyone else, but lacks the perception of how social interaction really works. He is like a child in an adult's body, unable to perceive and respond to the nuances of adult society: how to dress, what to talk about, how to behave.

If you don't have any true friends then you need to make a real effort, which may make demands on your time and ingenuity, to seek them out. But before you look for other people, look at yourself, and wonder if you could do anything to make yourself more appealing to others. Don't be too paranoid about this: even the most seemingly confident and popular people are insecure and nervous underneath; they just know how to control and hide it. If you can learn fake confidence, real confidence will often follow.

Making friends
Friends can be made in many ways, you just need the courage and stamina to go out there and do it. As explained above, to start with, you need to take a long hard look at yourself and ask yourself if you would like to be friends with yourself. If the answer is *no* then think of ways in which you feel you should improve yourself and/or your attitudes to make you a more attractive (not necessarily looks) person to be with. Someone who is happy and content with themselves is a very attractive person.

If you want to make a friend you have to proffer friendship. It is no good sitting in a corner and expecting people to come to you, you have to make an effort to reach out to them. For example if there are people whose company you enjoy at work, you could invite them round for dinner. Practise your skills as a host in your home environment, where you should feel at ease, and get to know them on a friendship rather than a work colleague basis, and see where it leads. You can get to know a lot about people as they relax and open up over the dinner table with a few drinks inside them. Hopefully, if the evening is a success, they will invite you to join them in a social environment, and you will get to know their friends. The more people you meet, the more chance you have of making some real friendships. You will never meet people sitting at home eating a tin of baked beans and watching the television. Just get out there and do something.

Try to meet people with similar interests. If you like sport and can join, for example, a tennis club or a golf club, you are half way there as you are meeting people who enjoy doing the same activity as you. If you have theatrical talents or merely enjoy being with people who have these talents, why not join an amateur dramatics society - you don't have to act, you could always be a stage hand and gain everyone's thanks for doing a job that they would rather not do.

Enrol in a college evening class and study a topic that interests you, whether it is the ancient Greek language or making flower pots. It is enjoyable to learn something new and to be with people who share the same enthusiasm about the subject. You will have lots to talk about and again it may lead to new friendships.

Many people find a social life for themselves when they join a Church, and take part in the various social activities organised by the community.

Get to know your neighbours and invite them round; proffer your help when you think they might need it. Be a friend.

You could join a reputable dining and social events organisation for single people, where everyone you meet will be looking to make new friends. If the club has sufficient members of a similar age and interests, you will probably land up with more new friends than you can cope with.

Staying friends

Keeping up your friendships takes up a lot of time and effort. Real friends make the effort to keep in touch with their friends, if only by telephone or by writing letters, and do not neglect their friends when life offers new opportunities, or cancel engagements when they are offered something better to do. Friendship is also a two way effort, it demands an equal responsibility from both parties for its upkeep. Relationships may come and go, but a friendship should be for life.

Reliability and loyalty are the basis of any friendship, but it is also important to be a good listener. Listening does not just mean making the right comments at the right time, it also means paying attention and taking an interest in what you are being told, and remembering it. As well as being sensitive to the needs of friends, it is equally important to have the ability to confide in them - most people will get fed up being with someone who is so secretive they will never reveal anything intimate about themselves.

It is important to understand your friends - their strengths and weaknesses - and to be able to tolerate their mistakes. It would be foolish to *drop* a friend every time they upset you. It is also important to learn how and when to say *no* to your friend's wishes and demands, because if you don't, and find yourself always saying *yes*, you could eventually feel used, taken for granted, and resentful of your friend.

Things that strain the relationship

Friendship has to be nurtured, and you have a responsibility toward a friend which you should never shirk. Don't be a good time friend who is always around when things are going well, and strangely absent when things are not - do not neglect a friend. Also do not use a friend by burdening them with your problems until they are exhausted by the sound of your voice, only to neglect them when your life takes a turn for the better. If you are constantly full of doom and gloom, off-loading your problems onto them without listening to see if they have any, your friend will soon decide that you are not their friend. Don't take your friends for granted.

Lending and borrowing can cause rifts between friends - you lend a friend some money and they never pay you back - you borrow someone's favourite keepsake and forget to give it back. You become resentful that they owe you money, they are too embarrassed to ask for their possession, and *bingo*, you're no longer friends. My uncle in law's favourite saying always used to be *Never a borrower nor a lender be*. Never lend anyone anything unless you are prepared to give it away. Always assume they will never give it back, and in that way you will never be disappointed, only I hope, frequently pleasantly surprised.

Strongly differing views on major political events can strain relationships. For example I knew a Serb and a Croat living in this country who were friends before the war in former Yugoslavia - now they won't talk to each other.

Strongly differing views on issues such as fox hunting, hanging, and racism could cause friends to lose respect for each other. Suppose someone who cares passionately for animals, and is appalled by the way veal calves are exported live in crates, goes out to dinner with a friend who immediately orders veal and proceeds to eat it in front of them - this could strain their friendship.

Personal issues such as two friends fancying the same person are not too helpful either. Also a friend would not seek to steal their friend's partner - there should always be honour amongst friends.

The pressures of work between friends who work together, could drive them apart. Unfortunately the old saying *You should never mix business with pleasure* is more often than not, true.

Trust
Trust is vital between friends. Once that trust is broken so is their friendship. One of the most precious possessions that anyone can give us is their trust, and we all have enormous responsibility not to betray it. Who needs enemies if we have friends that can do such a thing to us! For example, I think most of us have suffered at the hands of so-called friends and untrustworthy gossips, to whom we have imparted some information in confidence, only to find that to gratify their feelings of self importance, in that they know something that others do not, they have passed on the knowledge to most people we know. It would have been far easier for us to have told the rest of the world our secret in the first place, rather than suffer the embarrassment of finding out at a later date that other people have been discussing our personal details behind our backs.

No relationship between lovers can survive without trust. You have to be able to trust in the loyalty and decency of your partner, not to be *playing around* when you are not with them. Once that trust is broken, insecurity, jealousy and resentment sets in, and it is extremely difficult, and sometimes impossible, to rebuild it.

One of the most important rules of friendship is to always keep your promises. If you say you are going to do something, then do it. If you have any doubts as to whether you can keep your promise, then don't give it. If you regularly break commitments, your friends will disappear. It is no fun having an unreliable and irresponsible *friend* - it can only make you disillusioned and fed up.

A friend in need . . .

Real friends are always there in times of crisis - *A friend in need is a friend indeed*. If you suddenly won the lottery and became a millionaire you would acquire many new *friends* overnight. If you then lost all your money you would soon discover who your true friends were, as they would be the only ones left!

A true friend will see you through times of trouble or sickness, and if you come through such difficulties together you will have a much closer friendship.

Compromise

Always remember that life is a series of compromises, and if you are not prepared to compromise you could lose a friendship for the sake of your own ideas and principals.

Do not be stubborn in what you want to do. Listen to others and be prepared to go along with them. No one has the same interests - for example, you may be with a group of friends who want to go to the cinema but not everyone wants to see the same film. This could lead to arguments if they all push their feelings to the fore and the group could split. There has to be a sense of balance and compromise.

Complications

Making friends of the opposite sex
There is often an underlying assumption of a sexual motive in making new friends of the opposite sex, which is one of the barriers to forming true friendships. The film *When Harry met Sally* states, in effect, that men and women can never be true friends as the sex temptation will always get in the way. I personally do not subscribe totally to this theory, and am lucky enough to enjoy the company of several platonic male friends. Should you find that a friend takes a sexual interest in you, and you feel this could spoil the friendship, it is best to discuss it as openly as possible and make clear your intentions (or lack of).

Other complications

If you only look for friends who are a mirror image of yourself, this can sometimes lead to a somewhat dull and boring relationship. If we cultivate friends who have different attitudes and interests to our own, we learn a lot more about life and people. We all need someone who complements us so that together we offer more facets. Supposing a heavy rock music fan starts going out with a fan of identical music, they will not expand either of their lives. However, if a heavy rock music fan starts going out with an opera buff, and they learn to appreciate each other's tastes in music, then both their horizons will be expanded, and their lives will be more interesting and enriched.

Children can make life very awkward if they don't like your friend and he/she doesn't like them, and this will form a barrier to any relationship. You will need a lot of tolerance and understanding of both sides to try and combat this, and you may well find yourself being *piggy in the middle*. However, if the differences cannot be resolved, your children must come first - you can't choose your children, but you can choose your friends.

Your friends can be a problem if they don't like your new friend or, his/her friends! Again you will need to exercise all your understanding and ingenuity to try to sort things out, but in the end you have to ask yourself whether it is worth the effort, and who your real friends really are. A real friend will have enough regard for you to be tolerant, courteous and polite to any other friend of yours.

Dealing with complications
No friendship or relationship is without problems, and if you can learn to deal with them without running away, you will be far happier.

Try to look at your problems objectively and see if there is any way in which you can make them better. Try to see if there are any compromises to be made in order to make life less fraught.

Communication is essential in dealing with complications. If you have a problem then sit down and talk about it together. Don't go off and moan about your friend to other friends (which is a disloyal practise anyway), and make an effort to sort it out yourself.

As your friendship develops, so hopefully will your understanding of each other. You will learn how to treat your friend in order that they will respond well to you, and you will develop an insight into what pleases them and what annoys them.

Basically any problem can cause complications and it all boils down to how you deal with problems in life in general. You have constantly to work at any relationship, put all your efforts into it and don't leave at the first sign of trouble. The grass is not usually greener on the other side.

Chapter 3

Attracting Someone

This chapter is about the theory and practise behind searching for a partner and preparing for dates.

Positive thinking and self confidence
There is no point in even considering the prospect of attracting a partner if you feel unattracted to yourself. If you do not like yourself, how can you expect anyone else to? Unless you can think positively about yourself and be happy about the way you look, behave and react, you will have no self confidence, and self confidence is surely one of the key ingredients to attracting a partner. Initially I think you should invest some time in yourself and gain as much self knowledge as you can. Take a long hard look at yourself and decide what it is that you do not like.

Appearance
The first thing you will probably think about is your physical appearance. Your confidence may be at such a low ebb that you think you are positively ugly! Take heart, I have never met anyone who is completely satisfied with their looks. Top models are probably more self-critical in this respect than anyone. You need

to remember that whether or not you feel ugly, most people find love in the end.

Looks are only skin deep and the most important thing to cultivate is an attractive, caring personality who is sensitive to the feelings and needs of others. I think we have all at some point in our lives seen what we consider to be an ugly man or ugly woman walking down the street arm in arm with an exceedingly attractive partner, both obviously enraptured with each other, and thought *What on earth does he/she see in him/her?* The answer could be that the *ugly* person is extremely rich and the person on their arm is a *gold-digger*, but more often than not the attractive partner has fallen in love with a beautiful personality. The person we consider to be externally ugly could have an endearing disposition and a tremendous character. Here you might comment that if all it takes is money, you're off to make your fortune right away! This could be a very good thing for you to do as it might distract you from worrying about your looks and give you some confidence once you have made your fortune. On the other hand, it will probably take you quite a few years to achieve and it is therefore best to work on your character, personality and image at the same time as trying to make a fortune.

As far as your physical appearance is concerned it is best to start work on your body contours first. If you feel you are overweight, then before you do something about it remember that some people are naturally larger than others, and it may be that you are not over-eating but merely eating enough to maintain your natural body weight. Ask for honest opinions about your body size. Tastes vary, and while a slim person may be attractive to one individual, another may prefer a more rounded shape. It is very often fashion that dictates we should look thin, but fashion editors aren't everyone, and maybe some of us look our most attractive with our natural body weight . . . Marilyn Monroe certainly did!

Diets

If you do not think you are naturally built larger than others and want to lose weight, check that your weight problem is not a medical one. Everyone should seek their doctor's advice before embarking on a diet, because if you find that the problem is a medical one, you will have saved yourself a lot of wasted time with ineffectual dieting, and also the possibility of doing some actual harm to yourself.

Having established that you are fit and well and still want to lose weight, forget the word *diet*. It only focuses your mind on food, and food becomes an obsession. This could also lead you to the opposite extremes of anorexia or bulimia, and all the miseries and dangers that go with them, so please be careful. Just try to control your eating to three balanced meals a day with no eating in between. If you do fall by the wayside and have a sudden binge, don't get depressed and then eat even more to get over the depression!

Shrug your shoulders and try not to do it again. One useful tip I was once told, is that if you feel the urge to eat a box of chocolates or the like, just go and brush your teeth with toothpaste - you'll be amazed how it puts you off a potential binge!

Many of us, when we get miserable and depressed, eat to cheer ourselves up - comfort eating. This becomes a vicious circle as guilt feelings come in, making us feel even more depressed about the amount of weight we are putting on, which then causes us to eat even more. Many of us over-eat as a displacement activity - we all have countless things to do which we know we should or ought to do but, don't want to. How do we put them off? We eat and we get fat! Try to remember that *those who indulge - bulge!* Endeavour to write down, each day, a list of things you need to do and force yourself to do a few of them. It is amazing how crossing each one off in turn spurs you on to do the rest. You won't have time to over-eat. The rest of us probably over-eat out of plain boredom: you're on your own too much, start watching too much TV, nibble too much food, drink a little too much, get more and more lethargic, and in no time at all you are bulging at the seams - just living to eat and not eating to live.

As well as watching your intake of food try doing some exercise. Take up a sport, join a local gym, which will help subdue the hunger pangs, and the pounds will quickly roll away - again this is a good confidence gaining activity, plus you are meeting new people while you are doing it. Try to think thin and generally speed up your life with interesting things to do.

Image
If having sorted out your body you are still dissatisfied with your looks, try a change of image. If you can afford it, there are professionals who will suggest the right colours for you to wear; they will look through your wardrobe suggesting what does or does not enhance your image; they will advise you on fashion and what would look best on you; and finally, if you are female, they will do a make-up session, again advising you on the right colours for your skin and the way it should be applied.

The next person to visit is your hairdresser - maybe a new hairstyle is just what you need?

Another visit could be to the dentist. It is usually possible nowadays to have a perfect looking set of teeth, and some cosmetic tooth repairs can be done on the state.

Finally, if you are still worried that a particular feature of your face or body is unacceptable to you, and you will never feel confident until it is changed, you could consult a cosmetic surgeon. If after consultations you decide that this is the right path for you to take, do make sure that you fully understand and accept the complications that could occur, and double check that you have the best surgeon possible in this particular field.

Whatever image you decide to portray, you must feel comfortable and be able to portray your true self when you meet a potential partner. So many people, maybe unconsciously, put on an act to attract someone and wonder why, although their new relationship started off great, in the end they land up feeling disillusioned, dissatisfied, grumpy and nit-picking. Because they are not portraying their true self at the outset, the vibes they send out attract the wrong type of person and, by the time they settle down, relax and let their real character come through, they start to feel negative feelings because they are with the wrong person for them. Once again it is essential to take time off to gain some self knowledge as to your true self, and what your real needs are, not what you think they should be. Eventually this will enable you to recognise when you are starting to behave out of character, and then you can change direction to avoid making another mistake. If you truly know what you are looking for, what will make you comfortable and happy, and if you can also ascertain what your potential partner wants out of life, you will then have a better than average chance of finding out if you are both compatible with each other.

Things that are traditionally supposed to attract a partner

Money

Most people would like to feel that they will not be on the bread line when they link up with a partner, and would like to feel that they will at least be comfortably well off. They might well feel concerned if they found that you had massive debts and an unsound financial future. However, there are dangers in attracting someone who might only be attracted to what you can provide for them and the lifestyle that goes with it, rather than to you yourself. It is true that money will attract people to you, but are they the sort of people you would want?

Power

A powerful man is someone who very often attracts women, but often a powerful woman can be a complete turn off to a man. Women are very often attracted to success, which makes them feel safe and protected, with the prospect of a sound financial future ahead, whereas a man may possibly feel threatened by a successful powerful woman and feel he cannot compete or even keep up - he may well give up before he even starts. Power is possibly an advantage to a man, but a woman would be well advised to play it down at first, at least until she knows that the man does not have a problem with it.

Good looks

Most of us would like to feel we are good looking and will attract a good looking partner. However, there can be drawbacks if the person we are trying to attract feels we are too good looking and therefore out of their league. Most people want someone who is visually on an equal basis - in their *league of attraction*. We all know what is attractive to us, and in our minds we can be ruthless with ourselves as well as with friends and strangers, and we generally tend to stay within the same league - we will go for what we feel is comfortable and safe and makes us feel at ease. If we go for someone who is out of our league, we feel insecure. It is a bit like climbing a mountain - you can keep on going to the top but you might fall off. However if you settle for half way you'll probably be safe.

Very often a woman will distrust good looks in a man and choose someone with personality and presence instead, and a man may think that a very attractive woman might be a life sentence of keeping up with. As I think men are inherently lazy, they probably go for the easier option of a less attractive woman. Therefore contrary to popular belief, I feel very attractive people are sometimes at a disadvantage and should concentrate on making themselves look as approachable as possible, and also comfortable to be with.

Fame
Fame is of course a factor that will bring you instant recognition and attract many potential partners, but it will be a difficult exercise ascertaining whether your potential is attracted to you, or the celebrity image you are projecting.

Impressive possessions
Cars, yachts, houses etc. are merely worldly attributes that will attract many people to you, but you have to be sure that you are the foremost attraction. It is sometimes a good idea to introduce your potential partner to your acquisitions after you have got to know them well and formed some kind of relationship. Basically, the ordinary things in life are what you should be aiming for in attracting a partner.

Sense of humour
No relationship should be without it. The ability to laugh and generate laughter in others is possibly one of the greatest attributes anyone could hope to acquire. To be able to see the humour in the direst of situations and to be able to cheer people up instead of depressing them, is worth its weight in gold.

Being fun to be with
If you are a fun person, at peace with yourself, you will be amazed at how attractive you will be to others. If your body language indicates you are ease with yourself, others will feel at ease talking to you. Try not to be negative about things that you don't approve

of - always keep an open mind and listen to another's point of view. Just be laid back and try to give everyone around you a stress-free life.

Modesty

This does not mean you have to be a wimp . . . you can have a quiet assurance about you and your achievements without forcing them down someone else's throat. False modesty, however, is something to be avoided - it can be irritating when someone makes a point of deliberately playing down their achievements in order to induce you to praise them even more, and to take pains to reassure them as to how clever they have been.

Reasonable appearance and dress sense

Everyone wants someone who is well groomed - well turned out - it immediately catches the eye. Always look as good as you feel you can, after all, you never know who you might meet or where - some of the most successful liaisons have started out at the local supermarket check-outs!

Chapter 4

Communication between Men and Women

Over the past seven years that I have been running *Dinner Dates*, I have dined with over 25,000 single men and women, and have observed a huge amount of talk aimed at starting new relationships. Some of it has been admirable but some of it has been disastrous!

Where do you find him/her?
The short answer to this question is - anywhere. Therefore you should always be *on your toes* and look your best wherever you are, as you can never tell who is about to come round the corner.

Obviously some situations provide more opportunity for meeting a potential partner than others. Although many a liaison has started out over the frozen peas section at the local supermarket and it has turned out to be love at first sight, people are usually more susceptible to being approached when they are at leisure, for example on holiday, at a party, at a wedding, or at the gym or sports club. Public transport such as a train journey is also a good meeting place, maybe because of the boredom factor which causes people's eyes and minds to wander on to other things.

Many a relationship starts at work, however I would always advise against it as I do not think it a good idea to mix business with pleasure - there could turn out to be far too many complications if things go wrong. Joining a reputable dining and social events company for single people also provides marvellous opportunities, with the added peace of mind that you are safe-guarded against being introduced to a married man or woman with all the heart-ache that it may lead to.

You see someone you like, what do you do next?
The first thing to remember when you set out to talk to someone that you find attractive is that you have to make contact. Sometimes the simplest and easiest way is just to smile - it really is quite difficult to be unaffected by a genuine friendly smile, and it usually results in a friendly smile back to you. By smiling at someone, you are telling them that you are interested in them and find them attractive. By smiling back at you he/she is returning the compliment.

Eye contact can also be a fairly powerful way of contacting a potential's attention, and one method you could try is *the five second gaze and smile*. The reaction is usually instant, and they may well approach you. However, if it results in a glare, move on straight away.

If you can get through either of these first hurdles, it is by no means a guarantee to success, but at least you have created an opportunity for further contact.

The next thing to do is to try to open up a conversation, and here there is no point in agonising over what you should say - just say something, even if it is only *hello* to get the dialogue going. You will know within minutes whether your attentions are welcome or not - the tell-tale signs that they are not could be hidden yawns, eyes darting round the room, head rolling to one side or simply an unwillingness to converse back. If you recognise any of these signs, extricate yourself as soon as possible. Never feel rejected or put off by a rebuff - after all, we can't all be attractive to those we would like to be - just keep your dignity and retire gracefully. However, if he/she appears interested in you, wants to converse, seems unthreatened and relaxed with you, it will have been well worth the effort.

Never overestimate the situation; always be laid back and careful not to overplay your hand. Just because someone is enjoying your company, it does not necessarily mean they fancy you and would like to go out with you - they could already be in a relationship and are unavailable, but this is something you will need to ascertain during the course of the conversation.

Body language signs are exceedingly helpful in ascertaining whether your advances are welcome or not. Again the eyes can reveal much here - if he/she maintains constant eye contact with you, they're probably interested in you and what you are saying. If someone is not giving you their full attention and their eyes are looking everywhere except at you - forget it. By the same token if your eyes are scouring the room and not concentrating on them, they will forget you. If someone talks to you with their arms crossed and has a closed stance, they are holding back for whatever reason and are not relaxed in your company. On the other hand, should they appear relaxed with an open stance, you can gain confidence. Also, of course, you will feel intuitively whether you are at ease or not. Never put on an act to impress someone: it's hard work and eventually the mask will inevitably drop and the true you will emerge.

General talking advice

Always show interest in the person you are talking to. If you like their appearance, clothes, or smell, tell them. Never give false flattery that anyone can see through, but genuinely make the other person feel good and, even more important, comfortable. Everyone likes getting genuine praise, and if you make them feel good they are more likely to foster good feelings for you. It is essential not to use the same stock flattering phrases to everyone you speak with, especially on the same evening. They may well be friends who will get together (usually in the loo) to compare notes, resulting in mistrust of what you said, embarrassment to you and rejection from each of them.

Try not to be too inquisitive at first as to what the other person does for a living, where they live, etc. This sometimes puts a person on the defensive and makes them feel pigeon-holed. Keep the conversation more general.

Be a good listener - there's nothing worse than someone who talks non-stop about themselves, their likes and dislikes - it may well indicate to the person being talked to that at a later date you may not be interested in pleasing them and satisfying their needs. At the same time, don't be silent to the extent that it seems you have nothing to say, and maybe something to hide.

Don't be over the top, but don't be dull.

Don't dismiss what the other person talks about as being trivial, but at the same time don't be a people pleaser and pander to every word they say in an obsequious way. I once knew someone years ago who would make a statement about something and then, when the girl he was keen on voiced the opposite opinion, would immediately back track to fit in with her. This behaviour was very irritating to all concerned and did not help his cause with her at all.

Never force your attentions on someone, but try not to be backward in coming forward. What can you lose?

If you feel you need an alcoholic drink to give you some courage, have one. However do not go to extremes - it is very off-putting to be approached by someone who has had one or more too many, particularly when they start to make fools of themselves. Take just enough to loosen your inhibitions a little, but no more.

Concentrate on what the other person is saying because it is very unflattering later in the conversation if you repeat a question - this will show that you have not taken in what the other person has said and, your mind has been wandering away from them. This behaviour led to a disastrous situation one night at one of my *Dinner Dates* evenings. A man had been talking to a particular woman all evening and finally feeling he was on safe ground asked for her telephone number. She said,

'No!'

He asked, 'Why?'

She replied, 'You sat next to me in this same restaurant last year and asked for my telephone number. I gave it to you and you still haven't rung me!'

Sometimes it's not what you say but the way that you say it. At another of my dinner parties a girl was sitting looking rather bored, obviously being unsuccessfully chatted to by the men on either side of her, when the waiter came up to her. He looked long and deeply in to her eyes with his own beautiful limpid blue eyes and said in a voice which spoke volumes,

'Horseradish madam?'

I have not seen either of them again since that evening, and I gather they are both living blissfully together.

Whatever stage of the conversation you have reached, a sense of humour is essential - everyone likes a sense of humour and a laugh (however miserable they may look on the surface) - it helps break down barriers seen and unseen, and relaxes you both.

Always be positive - a negative and complaining attitude is a complete turn-off. Also don't start talking about your problems - I expect your potential has enough of their own which they don't want to add to.

Throw away your check list about the *perfect* person you would like to meet. This being does not exist. If during the conversation your potential feels you are checking off various points on a mental check list, he/ she will run a mile.

Come to terms with your age and don't waste your time in trying to attract someone who is unsuitable for you. Many people when they get older become obsessed with their age. As director of Dinner Dates I speak to many people on the telephone every day, and sometimes I feel like screaming when they say to me 'I look very young for my age' or 'I don't look my age' or 'I only get on with younger men/women'. In their anxiety to regain their youth or enhance their image with friends, they constantly seek a much younger person, which in my experience usually leads to unsatisfactory results.

Traditionally it has usually been men making the first moves on women rather than vice-versa, however nowadays I feel the tide is turning, and women are frequently to be seen taking the lead.

Men communicating with women

One of the main stumbling blocks to a man approaching a woman is the mood of fear that prevails today. There are so many horror stories in newspapers and on television at present that many women are naturally suspicious of advances from a stranger. Women feel a lot safer if the man who is chatting her up has been *vetted* in some way, e.g. he is an established friend of someone she knows. For this reason, if you can establish any link between yourself and the woman you would like to get to know, it is worth its weight in gold. If this is impossible, be constantly aware of potential fears and take things slowly and carefully to build up her confidence.

Women communicating with men

Women communicating with men is a vastly different ball game. Women tend to be more calculating in their approach, and contact is very often made indirectly through third parties. In a subtle way the woman *invites* the man to talk to her, making it seem like an achievement for him when she *consents* to go out with him.

Although nowadays it is becoming more and more fashionable for women to approach men and ask them out, and many men find it flattering, others feel wary, threatened, intimidated and trapped, especially if the woman is too pushy. The subtle approach of making the man feel he has done the hard work is therefore probably preferable.

Divorced women with children would be well advised to forget the word *we* initially - this can be dropped in later.

It can often be a disadvantage to be a very attractive woman because men may find you unapproachable. Many men are frightened off by an exceptionally good looking woman, and fear they would not be able to cope. If they think she could be a life sentence of hard work keeping up with her, they will probably go for an easier option. The answer here is to play down the good looks with your personality and conversation. Make yourself down to earth and approachable and keep the conversation ordinary but interesting. The more attractive you are, the more important it is not to overwhelm the man and make him feel exhausted at the mere thought of being with you.

Having successfully conversed with Mr or Miss Potential you need to ask them out. If you are a woman you could suggest a game of tennis or any other sport you may have in common, or arrange a dinner party and ask him to join you and your friends, or suggest meeting for lunch one day or a drink after work.

If you are a man you could also do any of the above, or ask her out to dinner, a concert, the theatre, the cinema - anything that you might have gathered she is interested in.

You will, however, need to get his/her telephone number, if only to confirm arrangements. Here I must tell you about a very novel way one of my members goes about it - he says it's foolproof.

During the conversation he asks the woman to write down her signature for him; he tells her how interesting it is and mentions he is into graphology, and how much he would like to do her signature analysis. He has a special computer programme for this and, if she would like to give him her telephone number they can meet when he has completed it, and give her the results. I've never known a woman to resist it!

Whichever sex you are, the solution to successful relationships lies within yourself. If you are a fun, relaxed, caring person, who is happy with themselves, you will be amazed how people will be attracted and drawn to you like a magnet - you may not even need to make any approaches yourself.

Chapter 5

Dating

Animals undergo all kinds of rituals before they mate with their chosen partner. Humans don't exactly parade their feathers like a peacock (although I sometimes see a similarity in modern fashions), relying on more complex and subtle techniques, and they date their partner to get to know them.

A brief history of dating
Dating has undergone many changes throughout the centuries: in the stone-age men used to bash their partner on the head with a club to impress them.

We then progressed to medieval times where the word *courting* was born. The royal courtiers didn't have to toil for a living, and used to spend their time going round trying to seduce (court) the ladies of the court.

In the 1900s customs became more controlled, and ladies were chaperoned throughout their courtship until the day they married.

Now that we live in liberated times anything goes - although with some men I wonder whether we have gone back to bashing women on the head again (mentally at least)!

Where to go on a date

Before choosing where to go on your date make sure that you are both happy with the location. There is no point in taking your date to a football match or a fashion show because that is what you would like to do, consider what would interest her/him. For example, if you know that your date is enthralled with cars then take them to a motor museum.

I think it is always a good idea to go somewhere where you can talk and get to know each other: restaurants and bars are ideal places. If you want to be slightly more imaginative, take them up in a hot air balloon and you'll be bound to talk to each other, if only out of sheer fright! If you and your date play golf, the golf course would provide ample opportunity to talk and get to know each other, whilst doing an activity you both enjoy.

Sometimes it's a novel idea to do silly things like spending the day at a theme park or going off to play *Quasar*, or if you really want to impress your date, fly them off to Paris for dinner.

If you are not so good at talking and would like to take things slowly at first, then arrange to go to the cinema, theatre or a concert which will give you a shared experience. When you first meet someone you have shared nothing, but once you have done something together the sooner you will be able to laugh and talk about a shared experience.

If the idea of a one to one date frightens you, then why not take the pressure off and arrange a double date with some friends. Again, if you are nervous about your date and feel you will need a drink throughout the evening to calm your nerves, it is no good turning up in your flashy sports car to impress her and risk losing your licence - it's better to turn up in a taxi.

If you feel your date is reluctant to go on a date alone with you, it may be less pressure on them if others are present. It might be easier to say that a group of you are going to see a film and would he/she like to join you or, you have been invited to a dinner party and would he/she like to accompany you.

Use your intuition when deciding where you should go and what you should do on a date, in order to enhance your chances with that person.

Handling the date

First of all you have to realise that everyone is nervous before they go on a first date, and it is natural to be so - you want to show yourself off to best advantage. You may quiver and quake so much with nerves that you become rooted to the spot and cannot even jump in the bath. The wonderful lady who looked like Barbara Cartland in a leotard, and who used to take my ante-natal classes when I was expecting my daughter, frequently told us that if we were in a situation we could do nothing about, (e.g. a traffic jam) and which was getting us in a state, we should *Drop shoulders girls!* I've never forgotten these words and they always work - dropping your shoulders instantly relaxes your tension. So when your nerves take you over, drop your shoulders, relax, and jump in that bath.

Give yourself enough time to get ready so that you are not late and in a fluster when you meet up. On the other hand don't give yourself so much time to prepare yourself that you are ready two hours early, pacing round the room and getting yourself in a nervous state.

Don't get your expectations up and expect too much from this first date. Make a determined effort to be laid back and normal, with the attitude that you will have a pleasant time, and get to know someone you like a little better than you knew them before. Be positive and confident in yourself - after all they would not have agreed to meet you if they had not liked you. Set out to be someone your date can feel comfortable with and trust - however up-tight you may feel, aim to put them at their ease.

When you meet, give a warm friendly smile and if possible, a continental kiss on the cheek. Then just say anything, such as 'Hi', to break the ice.

Talking

Hopefully when you first met your date and spoke to them successfully enough to invite them, or to be invited, on this date, you found out what their interests were. Armed with this information, you have a golden opportunity to *mug up* and do your homework on them, so that you can converse and ask intelligent questions when you meet on your date. If you know what someone's interests are, it is an excellent idea to encourage them to talk on the subject, as this will put them at their ease, making them feel more kindly disposed to you.

Try to see if you have any mutual interests such as a sport. If you find, for example, that you are both tennis players, this will give you a good excuse, if everything has gone well by the end of the date, to suggest that you meet up for a game. It's always good to find a non threatening way of inviting someone out again.

Although I am advocating that you should listen and let the other person talk about themselves, don't be too retiring about yourself to the extent that you might seem boring. Impart enough information about yourself to interest and whet their appetite, but don't go over the top. Always be modest and understated in what you say, it is far more impressive and will make them eager to find out more about you. Try to keep the conversation balanced at all times.

Never dismiss what someone says as being trivial, whether or not you disagree with it, but don't pander to every word they utter, like a *door mat*.

Never be negative and start moaning about your income tax, the government, politics, immigration - it is exceedingly tiresome for the other person, especially if they disagree with you and are too polite to tell you. Remember that other people may find such moans a bit of a *turn-off*.

Never start talking too much about your problems: everyone has enough of their own. If you do, you may be seen as yet another problem, and you may acquire the problem of never seeing your date again.

Sense of humour

Winston Churchill said, 'It is my belief, you cannot deal with the most serious things in the world unless you understand the most amusing'. Helping others choose to laugh, and standing back and seeing the ridiculous and absurd in almost any situation, is one of the most priceless gifts of all. Never waste a precious moment by feeling angry, when laughing feels so good. Laughter needs no justification, and if you can develop a sense of humour and induce your date to laugh, they will feel so good you will be well on your way to success. One of the most attractive things about a person is their sense of humour.

Body language

Observing the body language of your date will give you a clear indication of the way things are going.

The eyes can reveal much. The Victorians used to say that the eyes were *the mirror of your heart*. You can learn a lot by looking into someone's eyes, such as the chemistry, that indefinable something that makes two people attracted to each other, which may exist between you. If he/she has constant eye contact with you, then they are interested in what you are saying; if he/she is constantly looking you up and down this is also a positive sign; however if their eyes are darting round the room, looking at everyone except you, this denotes a lack of interest.

A relaxed smile is obviously a positive sign, while a frown is negative. A quick tight smile every time she/he realises they have not been paying attention, plus a vehement shake of the head to wake themselves up, is less than encouraging.

If someone has an open stance it means they are open to your advances and are not protecting their body space; if they sit tightly with their arms folded they are not relaxed, and you will find it difficult to get close to someone like that. Someone who sits sideways on, instead of facing you, is also hiding a part of themselves from you.

She may place her bag between you, thus defending her personal space; he may keep his hands in his pockets and demonstrate his unwillingness for physical contact. However, if they sit close to you, moving their hands freely as they talk, seem relaxed and unthreatened, they may be opening themselves up to you.

The tone of voice also gives a few clues - does it sound enthusiastic or does it sound bored?

Excessive fidgeting, hidden yawns, head rolling to one side, are also indicative of the way things are going.

Impressing

First impressions are always the most important, and the fact that you have already met your date and successfully persuaded her/him to come out with you, means that there must be something about you which impressed them. Therefore on this date you have to confirm, in their eyes, that their first impression was right, and you are an OK sort of person.

Someone who knows where they are at, and has an air of confidence and assurance about them without being pushy, is impressive. Someone who is genuinely courteous (for example a man who holds the door open for you, and gets up from his seat when you come back to the dinner table) because that is the way they normally behave, is a joy to be with.

As well as your general demeanour, the way you dress and present yourself is important too. Be slightly understated in all things, it is far better to be modest in dress as well as in manner.

You will also impress someone if you are happy, relaxed, and your own person with sense of calm about you. You can be fun, witty and amusing, and still retain this serenity which is most attractive. Never put on an act as the mask will eventually have to drop, and you might appear a fraud. The same goes for telling lies about yourself and the things you do, just to impress the other person.

If you are out to dinner your table manners are important as well, because you can learn a lot about someone's character by the way they behave at the dinner table. Never be boorish and uncouth by helping yourself to everything on the table before offering it to your partner. Don't grab the bread, wine, salt etc. as soon as you see it, as if you have starved yourself for days.

Don't brag or bullshit about your exploits and achievements, it is much better to be modest and self effacing. Also do not criticise others that you know to your date, as they might begin to wonder what you are going to say about them behind their backs.

Don't feel the need to prove yourself by letting slip that you are a millionaire or that you are a highly sought after individual. Let them find these things out for themselves. Indeed, if you are a millionaire, it is probably best to conceal the fact for the first few meetings, to avoid the possibility of someone getting *fond* of you for reasons other than yourself.

Whatever you do, don't hog the conversation and become boring. If you are out on a date playing tennis for instance, don't be a bore if you are a better player, by thrashing the other person at the game, to impress. You will get a lot further with them if you subtly let them score as well.

Consideration for others at all times is of prime importance.

Taking control of the conversation
Taking control of the conversation so that you can direct it in such a way that you can find out (in a subtle manner) whether there is any hope of a relationship of some kind between you, is a useful exercise to undertake.

Having encouraged the other person to talk about themselves, their interests, pursuits and achievements, you need to redirect the conversation to more personal matters, and try to get the other person to open up and give you a clue as to what they think about you. You could refer back to the occasion when you originally met, and reveal why it was that you felt inspired enough to invite them out, or accept their invitation. Hopefully they will respond with enthusiasm, telling you their thoughts and feelings at the time, and you will be able to gather whether you could be in with a chance.

If they are somewhat reticent, maybe things are not going so well and you will need to employ other tactics to regain their initial interest. However, I must point out here that many people prefer to be reticent about their attraction to their date for self preservation, and also because they don't want to appear to be a push-over. It is such a shame that we cannot all be honest about our feelings for each other, and that life often seems to be a series of playing games.

Assessment
At some point during the date, you need to assess whether the person with you is someone you would like to date again, and here I must stress, as I have done many times in this book, that this does not mean taking out your mental check list as to the *perfect* person you would like to spend the rest of your life with.

Perfectionistic ideals can paralyse your life. Looking for the *perfect* person can immobilise you and keep you on the side-lines of life, and prevent you from enjoying potentially pleasurable and promising relationships. It is no good setting your sights and standards so ridiculously high, because no human is completely perfect. God can be perfect, but we cannot.

Only a person who is committed to being non committed will do this, and he/she will end up being a very lonely person. Life is, and cannot be anything other than constant compromise. Look for the good points in people and develop on those.

Talking to someone and directing the conversation to reveal various facets of their personality and lifestyle, can help establish a picture of their whole person.

If you have definite dislikes that you could not possibly tolerate in another, then it is better to find out sooner than later. You may have strong religious views which they do not share; they may be racist and this would be intolerable to you; you may be a committed vegetarian who could not spend too much time with an omnivore; you may be a non smoker who is even allergic to smoke, whilst they turn out to be a chain smoker; they may have such strongly differing political views or views on life in general, from your own, that you decide they are not the person for you. Whatever it is that you discover in this person that you could not tolerate, it is best that you find out as soon as possible.

If, on the other hand, you enjoy their company, and find you have common interests and ideals, then I hope you will find a way of seeing them again and developing this relationship.

Chapter 6

Keeping the Relationship Going

Romance

What is romance?
Love is what makes the world go round, and romance is what makes a successful relationship go round. Too much romance could be taken for granted and thus spoilt; too little romance could starve the emotions.

Romance can be a little act, full of surprise, that fills you with feelings of warmth inside for the other person and helps kindle the flame of passion in a relationship. A romantic act does not have to be an extravagant gesture, just something that makes the other person feel special. A surprise single rose given from someone special in her life, can thrill a woman just as much as an expensive present. An occasional card that expresses your feelings and appreciation of your partner; a telephone call just to say *I love you*; a special kiss while you're dancing to your favourite tune - these and many more can titillate you both.

Romance can be a situation in which you share your, maybe as yet unspoken, feelings with the other person. A candlelit dinner for two; a moonlit sail; *holding hands at midnight watching a starry sky*, sitting on a hillside watching the dawn break - anything that gives you that glorious feeling of enveloping warmth, excitement, expectation, sharing and togetherness.

Music plays a large part in romance. Having a piece of music or a song that is special to you both and which reminds you of each other is so important, because each time you hear it, it will conjure up a multitude of feelings and memories. I still get wobbly every time I hear Barbara Streisand's recording of *Love Songs*.

Romance can invoke ecstasy and deeds of chivalry. One of the most romantic tales I have ever heard concerned two of my *Dinner Dates* members. They met at one of the dinners and had been going out together regularly when she celebrated her 40th birthday. Her girlfriends gave her a present of a trip to the far East and she asked him to go with her. He couldn't get away from work so she set off alone with her girlfriends. When she arrived she tried telephoning and then faxing him to no avail and, after a few days of this, she felt so miserable she went to her room, sat on her bed and had a good cry. After a while she noticed a box beside her on the bed; she opened it and inside was a paper ring with a note - *to be exchanged at a jeweller of your choice.* Just then, there was a knock on the door, and there he was dressed as a waiter, carrying a tray with a bottle of Champagne and two glasses. Within minutes he asked her to marry him!

Making an effort to keep romance alive
As with anything else in life, romance will eventually die unless you make a constant effort to keep it alive. Romance needs a lot of imagination and ingenuity to keep you and your partner's interest afloat.

Don't get lazy and let yourself go, slopping around in your comfortable old clothes all the time when you are both together. Occasionally surprise your other half with a dinner invitation, and then go to work and set the scene. Mood lighting with candles, mood music, Champagne or their favourite wine (providing your are not both tee-total) a light meal which will not tire you both out, and dress to kill.

You could go to a favourite restaurant that you know has live music, have a quick word with the band and get them to play *your tune.*

Surprise her with a bunch of flowers or an impractical unexpected gift.

Go and see a romantic play, musical, film or hire a romantic video to watch together, and just see how it can improve your love life. Even walking hand in hand in the park on a beautiful summer's evening, or cuddled up in front of a log fire on a winter's evening, can be full of romance.

The bedroom is an extremely important place, and relationships can die or flourish in them. Make your bedroom a special place where romance has a fighting chance to blossom. Make sure you have clean sheets on the bed, that the lights can be dimmed, and if possible use candlelight sometimes. Have soothing pictures on the wall, not your college certificates, use subtle colours for decorating the walls, and try gently scenting the air with a fragrant pot pourri. Don't just jump into bed each night and wait expectantly for the other person to follow. Make a conscious effort every now and then to seduce your partner into bed, and make it a tantalising night to remember. Also I cannot stress enough how personal hygiene is of paramount importance in an intimate relationship.

Sometimes we get too comfortable with each other causing familiarity to breed contempt, and without the added spice of romance, love can fade - never take your partner for granted.

Sex
Sex is of course a major component in the relationship, and without those underlying urgent feelings of needing your partner sexually, feeling satisfied and being able to satisfy your partner, your relationship does not have a rosy future.

Many relationships, at the beginning, are based on lust, and eventually love and real caring for each partner grows from this. Equally, many relationships start as a friendship, and as each partner grows to love and understand the other both mentally and physically, sexual attraction between them increases. A relationship that is based on friendship which grows into physical lust is possibly a more sound prospect for an ongoing successful relationship, rather than that which is based purely and solely on lust; but however the relationship started out, without a driving sexual need between you, problems will occur.

One of the first signs that something is amiss in a relationship is when one or both partners no longer desires the other. Immediately this happens you must sit down and talk about it, to ascertain whether or not there is a problem. Maybe your partner is tired and under stress, and is not physically able to give the passion they would wish to give, however if this is the case, they will still be giving you love and affection. If their feelings have changed for you, and they feel unable mentally to give the passion previously expressed, it is best as soon as possible to try to sort things out. When friendship between two lovers disappears, sex flies out of the window.

Just as romantic gestures may have become a habit and thus lost their novelty, so the novelty of sex might have worn off. As with any other aspect of the relationship, sex has to be constantly worked at, and a lot of ingenuity and effort is needed to prevent boredom. Never take your partner's sexual attraction to you for granted - never give up on the romance, and if necessary read a few books, and watch some sexy films for ideas - even consider making sexy videos of yourselves and see what it does for your sex life!

Staying friends with your lover

It is pretty nigh impossible to have a loving and fulfilled relationship with a partner unless there is a deep underlying friendship between you. Such a friendship will need constantly to be worked at.

Sometimes in a long relationship we get so close to each other that we have exactly the same opinions and tastes, we lose our individuality and maybe can't do anything or go anywhere without the other - this will eventually stifle your relationship.

If you are genuinely friends with your lover you will respect their individuality and not try to change them into a mirror image of yourself, or into what you yourself would like to be. Genuine friends have mutual trust, do not take liberties with each other, allowing the other person the freedom to pursue their own interests and see their own friends, as well as doing things together with mutual friends.

Genuine friends will listen to each other's aims and goals, support and encourage them, praise when necessary and share intimacies. If there are differences of opinion they will sit down and talk them through, to resolve them - there is always constant communication between them.

Friends will not set enormously high standards for their lover to live up to, which they themselves know they couldn't possibly do. They know that having a perfect partner, which of course does not exist, will not rub off on them and make them more perfect. Friends know the importance of compromise.

Lovers who are friends will always be thinking of new ways to please and stimulate the other. They like making each other happy and would not undermine the other's confidence with constant criticisms, just for one upmanship - that is an extremely unfriendly thing to do. They like making each other laugh, because it is stupid wasting your life being angry when laughing feels so good.

I must add here that if your partner has children from a previous relationship, it will be very hard to stay friends with her/him, unless you make an effort to be friends with their children. Children are very protective of their parents, and if they have seen them hurt before, they will need some winning over. It is up to you to make the advances of friendship - they are children, you are an adult.

Dealing with annoying habits

Everyone has habits that others don't like, and spending a large part of your time with someone means that you are bound to find out all their unusual habits. The problem here, of course, is how do you deal with them without getting resentful and uptight, and finally *blowing your top?*

I'm afraid it's the old word *compromise* that comes to the fore again. If you have similarly annoying habits, you could sit down and discuss them together, and maybe you could trade them off by giving up some of yours in exchange for your partner giving up some of theirs.

Sometimes it's best to hold your tongue and just live with the other's annoying habits and then, if they get too much for you, try shock tactics. An obvious one that comes to mind is in dealing with a thoughtless and inconsiderate partner who maybe never clears up after themselves. This person probably never does the washing up, leaves dirty cups and plates around, throws their belongings on the floor never thinking to pick them up, and has no idea how much hard work he/ she is causing their slavish partner - they just expect things to be done for them as their *right*. The answer here is suddenly to down tools and see what happens or, go away for a few weeks and see how they fend for themselves. You'll be surprised how the mess will eventually get on their nerves and they will be shocked into action, and there is a chance they might start being more considerate in other areas of their life as well! If this happens don't go back to your old ways (however much you love them and want to do things for them) - you may find you are appreciated more if you do less, and they might start helping you with your chores.

When your partner's annoying habits really get on your nerves, you think you can't stand any more and are wondering whether this relationship is worth the hassle it's causing you, sit down in a quiet place on your own and reflect on your partner's good points. Remember all the little things and loving acts they do, often unrequested, for you; ponder on the many times when you know you have driven them to the point of exasperation and they have *bitten their tongue*. Weigh up whether their good points outweigh their bad ones and maybe you'll see things in a better light - after all none of us is perfect. In the end you have to realise that we cannot and should never try to change another person; we can change ourselves if we really want to, but we cannot change others.

Fear
Sometimes when we are so happy with someone and we love them so much, we get terrified that it won't last and that we will lose them. In a perverse way we become our own worst enemy and, unconsciously, actually sabotage the relationship in various destructive ways. When the relationship eventually goes wrong we have been proved right, because we knew that it could never last. The stupid thing is that if we had not panicked, it probably would have lasted.

Sometimes when we are scared of losing someone's love we tend to give too much of ourselves, do too much for the other person and, in the end overwhelm and irritate them. The more you do, the more likely you are to lose. If someone feels you are totally dependent on them they may lose respect for you and eventually leave. Everyone likes to feel needed, but neediness is a complete turn off. Needing is based on trust, is openly reaching out and asking for support and expecting that the other will do their best to assist. Neediness is desperately asking for help and support because you don't have faith that you will get it. Neediness makes the other person feel unappreciated and drives them away.

If you are not fearful of the unknown, you will never be fearful of losing someone or something.

Fear of failure is a very powerful fear, and many of us are fearful of failing to make our relationship successful. Failure does not exist. Failure is only someone else's idea of how something should have happened or been achieved. If the relationship does not succeed, do not equate it with your own self worth, and never harbour any thoughts that you have failed as a person. Things just did not work out, for whatever reason, at that particular time with that particular person.

It is probably best, in a relationship, not to give 100% of yourself - try to keep 10% back. Then, if the relationship does not last, you will not have lost your whole self completely, you will not feel entirely worthless and will be able to cope with life on your own. Too often people are devastated by the break-up of a relationship because they gave all of themselves to their partner and are left feeling completely empty and worthless when it is over. Consciously maintaining just a little of your independence within the framework of a relationship is like having a lifeboat on a ship. If the ship sinks, you won't go down with it because you can still float in the smaller lifeboat. Therefore develop hobbies, friends and interests outside of those involving your partner, and don't selflessly dote on your partner constantly. Try to be one of two whole people, rather than half of a completely unified couple. This is not easy to achieve, but it is a safe and strong recipe for long term success and survival.

To combat fear, you need the internal security of trusting in yourself to handle any problems that might come your way. If you are a rock of self esteem, the world may tumble around you, but your inner strength will make you survive. If you have trust in yourself you will be able to try anything and never fear having to explain yourself or your actions.

Jealousy

Jealousy is usually an insecurity in ourselves, and a feeling that we are worth a lesser amount of love than others, and that other people are more important than us. Many people are neurotically jealous and so insecure in themselves, that they see a potential threat in anyone their partner shows an interest in, or even talks to.

To rid ourselves of jealousy we need to recognise that it is a put-down of ourselves, and that if we love and believe in ourselves, we don't need the love and approval of others to give us a sense of value. Jealousy is allowing the other person's behaviour to cause you emotional discomfort. If you really liked yourself you would not allow yourself to get upset if your partner chooses to be with someone else. It is their choice and absolutely no reflection on you or your worth. There is no point in upsetting and driving yourself mad in thinking 'what's wrong with me?' or 'why aren't I good enough for him/her?' It is just your partner's choice at the time and, again I repeat, no reflection on you. Jealousy is yet another wasteful emotion that prevents you from enjoying the present, which of course is always the most important moment of your life.

Jealous people are often very possessive people and, strangely enough, I have often found that jealous people are often *playing around* themselves; they transfer their guilt onto the other person by convincing themselves that they are up to no good as well.

Jealousy is also a lack of trust, not only in ourselves but, in the other person, and no relationship can survive without trust on both sides.

I think we all have a responsibility towards our partner to make a conscious effort at all times to minimise the chance of jealousy occurring. By this I mean that we should be open and honest about what we are doing and not try to hide things in order, mistakenly, to keep the peace. If you behave in a secretive and underhand way, you will eventually make even the most easy going partner insecure and then jealous. Always remember, *be sure your sins will find you out.*

You should start a relationship without excess baggage. This means getting rid of predatory ex-girlfriends/boyfriends who still hanker after your love, even though you may need them to boost your ego, or because you are someone who always has to have someone on the side-lines as a safety net in case the relationship should go wrong. Although you may be a very clever and deceitful person who covers their tracks well, your partner will eventually pick up on vibes, become insecure and potentially jealous. If only people could keep their excess baggage as friends and introduce them to their present partner, and every time they feel like meeting up innocently with them on a friendship level could be open and honest about it with their partner, so much hurt, misunderstanding and strife could be avoided.

Boredom

I was at a party recently, and someone made a statement that I cannot get out of my mind - *Boring people get bored.* This is so true! People who are not boring do not allow themselves the self indulgence of getting bored, they will always find something with which to amuse themselves or someone else.

Very often boring people have so much time on their hands with so little to do, that they spend a large proportion of their time thinking. They tend not to use their thoughts wisely and, instead of questioning their own character, getting to grips with their own inadequacies and finding ways of improving themselves and making everyone's life around them more pleasant, they tend to dwell on the inadequacies of others. They may spend their lives moving from place to place and meeting new acquaintances, but in the end they will usually find fault with the location and people because they cannot escape themselves. At some point we all have to be realistic and realise that if our life constantly follows a pattern with which we are dissatisfied, the answer must lie within ourselves. We cannot always blame others and expect them to wave a magic wand and put our life to rights. We need to stop expecting others to give constantly to us while we just take. So, look into your bad points, appreciate other people's good points, stop being boring and one of life's takers, and start living and giving.

In a relationship do not allow yourself to slip into becoming a boring person who lets the relationship go stale. If you make a conscious effort not to be boring you will always think of things to talk about and do with your partner rather than sitting back and expecting them to amuse you.

Never expect your partner to provide all the inspiration. Be responsible for yourself and do not expect the other person to live your life for you.

Be original and keep the relationship exciting and interesting, and try not to fall into routine habits. For example in a new relationship you may delight your partner by buying her a bunch of flowers. If, however, you do this regularly each week it becomes a habit, it becomes expected and loses its novelty value. If you regularly go to the same restaurant each week, that will eventually become boring. Think of new things to do and seek ideas from newspapers or magazines. The old saying that *variety is the spice of life* is very apt. Go to the theatre, concerts, films; go away for weekends in the country (if you live in a town) and weekends in town if you live in the country; visit places of interest such as museums; play sports and watch sports together; go out to dinner and give dinner parties; learn a new dance together such as Ceroc; go on walks or climb mountains; listen to music together; do home improvements - do a variety of things together but not with regular monotony. Try not to get into regular routines which could eventually bore you both senseless. Boredom is debilitating and unhealthy, and sometimes you need to add a little spicy uncertainty of new experiences to get rid of the routine and sameness in your life.

Every few months sit down together and re-evaluate your relationship. Set new guide lines, because not only is life constantly changing - we are as well.

I often feel that although one should be with a partner who shares similar interests and ideals to some extent, if you are both too similar and a mirror image of each other, life could get rather boring, without extreme efforts to stop it being so.

Put some energy into your lives, develop a curiosity about what is happening around you, and create new opportunities for doing, thinking, feeling and living.

Resisting other attractions
Be satisfied with what you have and look but don't touch. You will be attracted to others of the opposite sex because you are only human, but make a conscious effort not to do anything about it. Whilst a change to someone different may seem to be an improvement on your current relationship, we are usually attracted to the same type and this sameness may not be apparent at the first meeting. The grass usually doesn't turn out to be greener and you run the risk of losing someone very precious in your life.

Don't put yourself in the way of temptation. For example don't go to a party on your own or on holiday on your own - try to go as a couple. If people make advances to you don't deny your partner; although you may find it flattering, don't lead the other person on, and make it quite clear that you are part of a twosome.

If you are at all happy in your relationship, don't jeopardise it for the sake of a fleeting fling. It is far too easy to look elsewhere for what is missing in your relationship, instead of working hard to get things right between you.

Understanding each other

I recently read that although men and women speak the same words, what they mean when they say those same words is so vastly different that they might as well be speaking in different languages, and even have originated from different planets! We also all expect our partners, if they love us, to react and behave in the same way as we, who love them, would. If only men and women were able to accept and respect their differences how much easier life would be.

For example, men like solving problems whereas women feel a lot better by talking about them. When a woman has had a terrible day and proceeds to tell her partner all about it, she does not want him telling her she shouldn't be upset and offering solutions to any problems she may have. This will only irritate her and eventually could lead to a row. What she needs is for him just to sit there, listen, make appropriate sympathetic comments and maybe put his arm around her. When she has finished telling the tale, she will feel so much better for having had him listen to her problems, she will be extremely grateful for his support and her feelings for him will be enhanced. She needs a listener, not someone who tells her what to do.

When a woman resists the man giving her solutions he may well feel mistrusted, unappreciated, and eventually stop caring and being willing to listen. When a man resists a woman giving him solutions, she may well feel that he doesn't care, he doesn't respect her, and she may stop trusting him. This is a fundamental dilemma that can only be overcome by mutual understanding of what the other person really wants, so remember men feel better by solving problems, and women feel better by talking about problems.

Men are frightened of failing and not seeming to be good enough or competent enough when dealing with a woman's problems and find it hard to listen. If the woman is not satisfied with his advice he may well feel a failure inside, which supports his deepest fear that he is not good enough. When a woman tries to comfort a man and help solve his problems, he feels she doesn't trust him to deal with them on his own and he then feels controlled. A man will only ask for help and advice when he has done all he can on his own, and even then a woman has to be careful not to let him feel he has lost his sense of power or that he is being pitied.

Men like to be alone when they are upset, whereas women want to be loved, cherished, and supported when they feel upset. Many men experience emotional difficulties because they have been to school where they were taught that men keep a stiff upper lip and never cry. Women need constant reassurance and should not be criticised for this, just as a man should not be blamed for needing to withdraw sometimes. I feel that a lot of men should learn how to give themselves more, and that women should learn how to receive that giving, because many men are afraid of giving, and many women are afraid of receiving.

One of the biggest hurdles for a woman is to understand why, and also to support a man who isn't talking to her. Women often tend to imagine the worst when a man goes silent - he's gone off me and he's about to leave. However, many men go silent because they need to think about problems in their life and quietly find the solution, whereas a woman would probably do the opposite, and phone up all her friends and try to talk her problems through. Sometimes when a man goes silent he may be stressed, with the need to cool off and find his control again and avoid saying something he may regret. Often when a man gets too close to a woman all his warning bells go off and he has to retreat before he can get closer. He pulls away to fulfil his need for independence and control, and when he is fully stretched he springs back again. If he is not allowed that freedom to pull away, he will never get a chance to feel strong desires to be even closer.

The worst thing a woman can do when a man pulls away is either physically or mentally to follow him. He needs to be on his own to come to his own decision to bounce back, and any pressure from the woman will drive him further away. Very often a woman will punish the man when he comes back, by physically pushing him away for making her feel unhappy, or mentally by going cold and not talking to him or allowing him to listen to her. This is actually the time that both of them should talk but, the woman (who does not understand why her man left her) is often very afraid to in case he runs off again.

Women tend to confuse men sometimes because, due to their hormonal cycles, one minute she will be strong, glowing with happiness and love, and shortly afterwards she will be unhappy, depressed, needy and possessive, for no apparent reason. A lot of men expect a woman's emotions to be stable and cannot understand when she suddenly goes under. At this time a woman does not want him to tell her to pull herself together and say that she shouldn't be upset - she needs support and a listening ear, and then she will come up again.

Men want space and the right to be free whereas women want understanding and the right to be upset. If a man could support her need to be heard, she could then support his need to be free.

General advice on keeping the relationship going
In any relationship you need a mixture of independence and dependence. You need to have the independence of your own bank account, hobbies and interests as well as depending on your partner for support and appreciation. It is important to support and appreciate your partner's talents in a positive way and, it is important also, to have a quarrel or even a shouting match with your partner if you are really upset with them. If you just get withdrawn, sulky, grumpy and silently angry, you are suppressing your negative feelings. Sometimes when you frequently suppress your negative feelings, you suppress your positive feelings as well, and the relationship gets endangered. It is far better to let out your feelings, whether positive or negative. It is always better to drag problems out of each other as soon as they occur and get to grips with them, rather than let them fester and become even greater problems. Be honest.

It is vital to communicate with each other and talk about the good things between you, your problems and worries. Once the communication is under way, it is so important constantly to negotiate and compromise. For example, it is no good if one partner is always off doing his/her *own thing* at the expense of the other - this can only lead to resentment.

To communicate, negotiate and compromise, you need to spend time together, and if you don't spend time together you may grow apart. Our grandparents had an advantage over us, in that I think life was less stressful and busy in their time, and they could spend lots of time with each other. Nowadays there is so much to do, we are so tired out working too hard trying to make ends meet, that we do not have enough time for each other, or for our families. It is a very sad reflection on modern day living.

Not only do you need to communicate with words, you need to communicate by touch. Many people find this extremely difficult because they may have been brought up in a family where you did not openly show affection for each other. The *touching* part of them has been suppressed and they might even convince themselves that because they cannot openly touch and show affection for their partner, they are not in love with them. This person needs to review his/her life and question whether they have ever been able to show affection for anyone - mother, father, sister or brothers. If they have not, then they need to start to learn, with their partner's help, how to sit close, how to hold hands, and how to put an arm around their partner in full view of the public. Once they have overcome the initial embarrassment, awkwardness, unfamiliar feelings that this will engender, they may find that being able to show affection is not that difficult or alien, and that being able to do so will unlock all kinds of inhibitions, and enrich their lives - who knows, they might even enjoy it!

Allow your partner to be themselves whether or not their ideas and opinions coincide with yours. Never try to suppress someone else's ideas or opinions just because they do not suit yours. By all means voice your opinions, but respect the fact that no one can conform to the perfect stereotype you may have built up in your mind, and we are all different. If you do not treat your partner with courtesy and respect, however much you may disagree with them, it is unkind and unfair, and can only lead to disaster. Always be open minded and able to see all points of view and, having considered everything, be adaptable. Life is a constant learning process and sometimes the learning, adapting and changing will bring chaos, but out of this chaos will come growth.

None of us has the right to undermine our partner's confidence. Always make constructive criticisms rather than destructive ones. For example instead of saying, 'You never take me out!', why not say, 'Wouldn't it be nice if we went out more often?'

The greatest personalities in our history have been those who can recognise when they are wrong, and say sorry. Be able to say sorry to your partner when you are wrong, and always be able to wait for your partner to say sorry to you.

Compatibility
If you spend your life worrying about whether your relationship is right or not, whether you are

compatible enough to keep the relationship going, you could drive yourself and your friends mad. If you constantly ask friends or even passing acquaintances whether this is the right woman/man for you, they will eventually get so exasperated, that they will tell you to leave her/him if it is that difficult to make up your mind. You must never put the responsibility of making such a personal decision onto other people.

You really have to relax and stop thinking about it, because if you don't, things will fall apart anyway whether the relationship is working or not. People find each other in so many random ways, and there are so many varieties and combinations that can work - it is just not worth thinking about.

If you are happy together more than 50% of the time you are doing well, so don't probe, analyse or question why - just accept it and be grateful. No one can ask more than to be happy with their partner and, however it happened, however unlikely a couple you may seem to be, you are most probably compatible if you enjoy being with each other. Put away your relationship magnifying glass.

Is it worth making the effort?
If you really like your partner, find them sexually attractive, feel happy and comfortable with them, even if you haven't yet recognised whether you are in love with them, yes it is definitely worth a lot of effort. There is so much to be gained mentally and physically

from a happy relationship, that you would be foolish not to try your utmost to make it work. Whatever differences you may have, unless they are completely insoluble, can usually be worked through if you have the determination to do so.

However many available people there are out there to chose from, it is still extremely difficult to find someone you feel happy and at ease with. Most relationships will start out well but, eventually every relationship will have its problems, because we are all difficult human beings. Just stop picking on all the bad points and start appreciating the good ones. Life is too short to keep chasing around after an impossible dream when you could possibly have something very special and worthwhile right under your nose.

If, on the other hand, you are really unhappy in each other's company, you no longer find each other sexually attractive and are constantly quarrelling, it probably is not worth the effort.

Making the effort

Always strive to make your partner feel good in themselves, and be understanding and supportive when they are down. Recognise your differences and accept them, so long as you are still happy with the rest of your relationship.

Make an effort to keep yourself attractive and in good shape - don't get lazy and complacent and let yourself go to pot.

Make a constant effort to keep life stimulating and interesting - don't let your relationship get boring.

Try to control your annoying habits and be tolerant of your partner's.

Many problems occur in the car, when one partner is driving and the other is map-reading. Make an effort to recognise the fact that although your partner may be brilliant at some things, they may not be the world's best map-reader. It is useless to fly into a rage every time they take you down the wrong way; it is far more constructive to have taken responsibility yourself, and made an effort to study the map before setting out. Getting angry will not make your partner better at map-reading, and you will only succeed in confusing and upsetting them, making matters worse. Also, make a supreme effort not to be a backseat driver. If your partner's driving upsets you, then offer to do the driving yourself. Backseat driving is not only disorientating and upsetting for the driver, it is downright dangerous and causes accidents.

Always make an effort to be open and honest about what you are up to, to your partner. In this way you will gain their trust, make them feel secure in the relationship and thus avoid potential jealous feelings in them.

Make an effort to respect each other's independence and space and try to communicate your needs to the other person. If you don't ask, you don't get. Always ask in a non demanding and direct way - you cannot expect someone to read your mind and it is better all round to spell out your wants. You must be prepared though, if you ask for something to accept a *no*. Never feel rejected if you get a negative answer - if you accept that your partner has the right to say *no*, they will remember that, and you will be more likely to get a *yes*, the next time you ask. If you deny your partner something for a long time and then eventually give in, you may find that it is too late - they don't want it any more and may feel extremely resentful towards you.

Try to add a little romantic sparkle to your lives and keep re-kindling the flame of your relationship.

Make a real effort not to be picky, critical and disgruntled, and learn to control immature temper tantrums - try your best to make life as pleasant as possible for those around you. Try not to slag people off and grumble about them behind their backs - if you can control this tendency, it will make you a far happier person and will also help your relationship.

Make an effort to include your partner in as many things as possible and develop mutual interests. In this way you will help to avoid the possibility of growing apart at a tangent.

Make the most of what you have got, appreciate it, and make a supreme effort to avoid temptations which could destroy it.

A relationship based on love, is one in which each partner allows the other to be what he chooses, with no expectations and no demands. It is a simple association of two people who love each other so much that each would never expect the other to be something that he wouldn't choose for himself. It is a union based on independence, rather than dependence. **Dr Wayne W. Dyer.**

Chapter 7

Marriage

A character in *Four Weddings and a Funeral* stated that he believed there comes a time in every relationship when the couple runs out of things to talk about. At this stage they decide to get married, and suddenly they have enough to talk about for the rest of their lives.

Why people marry - the right and wrong reasons for getting married

I would like to think that most people get married because they fall head over heels in love and, having thought long and hard about it, feeling that it will last forever, want publicly to confirm their commitment to each other. Unfortunately this is not always the case and far too many people land up in the Divorce Courts because they got married for the wrong reasons. Although it is relatively easy to get the decree nisi and decree absolute in divorce proceedings, the emotional and monetary upheaval and trauma, for all concerned, is extremely difficult. In contrast, I sometimes feel it is far too easy to get married, and I would like to see it made more difficult.

Maybe it would be a good idea if would-be brides and bridegrooms had to attend at least two official compulsory counselling sessions to ascertain whether or not they really understand what they are letting themselves in for, and all its implications. This would help many a couple who fall in lust, marry on impulse and live to regret it later. Also it would highlight many illegal *marriages of convenience* and appropriate action could be taken. I recently read in the newspaper that a certain Registrar stated that the majority of couples he married did not even know each other's names, and after the ceremony he frequently witnessed money changing hands.

There is much talk about a woman's *sell by date*, and many women in their early thirties feel pressurised into marrying any available male before it is *too late*. They may well have spent the preceding years concentrating on building up their careers, and not attached enough importance to their personal life. Suddenly their biological clock starts ticking over and they are desperate to have a mate and a child. I personally feel they should relax and stop worrying because with modern day obstetrics it is now possible to have a first baby in relative safety when you are forty. However most men and women have not been brought up to think this way, and men also feel the pressure to choose a young woman with whom to start a family. Maybe these days life has swung too much in the direction of careers and achievements, and we have lost sight of our own personal priorities and what is really important in life.

Many people are pressurised into marriage by their married friends who are either so blissfully happy they wish their friend to be in the same state, or are not *happy with their lot* and are jealous of their friend's freedom.

Families can exert tremendous pressures if they feel it is socially correct to be married at a certain age, or that it is wrong for two people to live together out of wedlock. Parents can sometimes be desperate to be grandparents, and they will exert pressure on their children to get married. Also in some cultures one has to get married, and marriages are *arranged* by the parents.

Many men are pressurised into finding a wife because their job requires them to do so, if they wish to progress up the promotional ladder. Many women feel they have to get married because they are pregnant, and even if they are not in love with the father, will pressurise the father into marriage. The man will often harbour resentments which will be brought up at any available argument, and the marriage will often fail. This can cause more heart-ache and problems to the parents and child than if they had made the decision to live apart in the first place.

With reference to the word *independent*, some people, because of the way they have been brought up by over-anxious or over-bearing parents, are very dependent. They find it difficult to make their own decisions and organise their own lives, and feel the pressure to attach themselves to someone else in marriage who will hopefully do it for them.

Someone once said to me that if faced with a choice, you should marry someone you like rather than someone you love - the liking will last for ever, the love may not!

However pressurised you may feel in deciding whether or not to marry someone, don't do it unless you really want to. Sometimes if you can forget the worries and reject the pressures, relax and just enjoy your relationship without thinking about the future, you will wake up one morning knowing what is the right decision for you.

Is it best to live together as a married couple before tying the knot?
Sometimes it is, sometimes it isn't.

Reasons for
Living together for a trial period with a view to eventually getting married can be a good and useful exercise to undertake. When you are dating someone, even if you spend time at each other's places, you tend to see their better side. If either of you feels irritated

and frustrated with the other you can retreat to your own patch and restore your equilibrium. If you start living with that person you will have the opportunity to find out whether your relationship can cope without having your *bolt-holes*. Living with someone will mean that you experience a lot more of their worse side, their annoying and irritating habits, again giving you the opportunity to decide whether or not this is what you really want, before deciding to tie the knot.

If at the end of your trial period you have weathered the storms and are still blissfully happy with each other, this will be a good foundation for your marriage plans. If this has not proved to be the case, and your relationship is falling apart under the day to day strain of living together, thank goodness you waited before tying the knot.

Reasons against
If you live with someone rather than being married to them, it is far too easy, at the first sign of any problems, to just *up and leave* rather than working the problem through - you always have a get-out clause. Although the majority of teething problems you will inevitably experience when two independent people start sharing the same space can usually be overcome, in a *trial marriage* these often get notched up as points against a final commitment.

You may find that you are so happy living together that you don't want to *rock the boat* by entering into marriage. If this is what you both want then all is well and good. However, if one partner is happy with the situation and the other wants the commitment of marriage, this can be a recipe for disaster. The partner who wishes to marry will start to lose confidence and feel insecure. In order to goad the other into making a commitment, they may create, sometimes not consciously, situations for the other to prove their love for them. In extreme cases, they may even start seeing someone else to provoke jealousy and a showdown.

Can asking your partner to marry damage the relationship if refused?

Yes, of course it can if the answer is a definite *no* with no chance of the person being asked changing his/her mind at a future date.

However confident you may feel about your loved one's emotions toward you, it still takes a lot of courage to lay your feelings and intentions on the line and ask him/her to marry you. If you have misjudged the strength of their feelings for you and they are not yet emotionally ready to commit themselves to you, they may well feel the situation has got too intense and *run a mile*! If having bared your soul to your partner and asked them to marry you and they refuse, you may probably feel rejected, and disinclined to continue the relationship.

If the refusal is because your partner does not feel ready at that particular time, for whatever reasons, to commit themselves to you, and they indicate that they would like to be asked again at a future date, there is some hope of repairing any possible damage.

I strongly feel that you have to be absolutely sure of your ground before you *pop the question*, as this particular question will completely change the whole basis of your relationship.

When/how best to propose?
The best time to propose is when you feel absolutely sure that this is the course you wish to take. Also I must mention here that although it has traditionally been the man who proposes to his girlfriend, it is now socially acceptable for a woman to propose to a man.

Everyone likes a bit of romance, especially at a time like this. There will never be such an opportunity to go so completely overboard on the romantic stakes. Indeed, forgetting the romance and asking a casual 'How about us getting married then?' whilst watching a football match on the television, might well leave your partner feeling somewhat cheated. This is a big occasion for both of you and should be treated as such. A romantic candlelit dinner for two would be an ideal setting, and whilst hand in hand with each other you raise your glasses of Champagne to drink a toast you could say with feeling, 'It would make me the happiest man/woman alive if you will marry me' or simply 'Will you marry me?' Even the good old fashioned formula of going down on bended knee and asking,

'Darling, will you marry me?' might not go amiss! Make the most of it and give yourselves a romantic memory to cherish in later years.

The mechanics of the wedding

There are many ways to get married - you can choose to have a traditional *white* wedding followed by a reception attended by friends and relatives, which can be simple or grand, or a registry office ceremony, with a handful of guests present, also followed by a reception if you wish. Many women cherish dreams of walking down the aisle in a beautiful white dress, and the ceremony that goes with it, and would feel they had missed out if they didn't have it. Many men feel inhibited by such elaborate proceedings and would rather opt for a registry office wedding if they are not too bothered about the religious aspect.

If you are Jewish you may choose to have your marriage solemnised in a synagogue or private house. Whatever the religion, many couples opt for the plainer wedding for financial reasons. The cost of a full-scale church wedding is now thought to average more than several months' wages for the average wage earner, and however this cost is shared between the couple and or their families, many couples feel they would rather have an inexpensive wedding and put the rest of the money towards their future.

Second weddings

If you have been through a divorce and wish to re-marry in a church, it is vital to check the rules regarding re-marriages with the clergyman. Some religions do not recognise divorce, or may require very strict formalities to be adhered to. Much will depend upon the denomination of the church in which you wish to marry.

Wedding Preparations

1. Announce your engagement
2. Decide on the form of ceremony you would like, and when and where it should take place.
3. Choose a venue for the reception for that day - this may be in a hall, hotel, marquee at home etc.
4. If you are having a church wedding, discuss the details of the ceremony with the minister - the style, order of service, the choir if desired, the hymns, the music to be played, and possibly bell-ringing. Find out about the fees, and ask if your guests may take photos or videos in the church and throw confetti in the grounds of the church. The minister may also wish to counsel you both about the significance of a church wedding, and ask if you would like to attend a marriage preparation course to take a look at all the broad issues involved.
5. Go to see the local Registrar as soon as possible if you are going to have a civil wedding. Find out the legal formalities and how many guests can be accommodated at the ceremony, and whether photos, videos and confetti are allowed.

6. Draw up a list of guests and send the wedding invitations out at least six to eight weeks before date of the wedding. These are traditionally sent out by the bride's parents unless someone else is hosting the wedding e.g. the bride and groom.

7. Choose the best man, bridesmaids and pages (if desired)

8. Prepare a wedding list for anyone who wishes to consult it - it is usually a good idea to employ the services of a large store where you will chose the items you wish to be given, and guests can peruse the list and order either in person at the store, or by telephone.

9. Write thank you letters for all gifts received.

10. Choose the wedding ring or rings.

11. Choose your wedding dress (do not let the groom see it before the wedding service) and choose the bridesmaids' dresses and pages' outfits if you decide to have either or both of these.

12. If you are the groom, order or buy your outfit. The best man, ushers and both fathers should dress with the same degree of formality as yourself.

13. Order the flowers - bouquets or posies for the bride and bridesmaids, buttonholes for the male principals, and displays of flowers for the church and reception.

14. Engage a professional photographer and video firm (if allowed by the minister).

15. Order the wedding cars if needed.

16. Announce the forthcoming wedding (time, date, venue) in a newspaper a few days before the chosen date.

17. Arrange the honeymoon.

18. If desired, arrange your stag party or hen party and, make sure you will have enough time after the event to be fully recovered and looking and feeling your best for the big day.

Married life together

One of the strongest recollections I have, immediately after I got married, was the difference in other people's attitude toward me. No longer was I his attractive *bird* invited along everywhere as one of the *lads*. I was suddenly respectable, and a wife, and I was treated as such. Gone was so much of the camaraderie of his male friends, and indeed a lot of the time I was treated with suspicion as they watched what they said in front of me. This came as a tremendous shock to me and took many months of heartache getting used to. Now I am sure that most people's reactions will not be as extreme as this, but their attitudes will change.

Getting married can sometimes be like joining a club and you will find many new doors and opportunities open up for you.

Marriage should be a new adventure to embark on, enabling your relationship to grow and let you go forward in life together. A marriage should be constantly worked on - never get complacent and *let yourself go* - always be considerate to the other's feelings - never stop striving to improve the relationship by your own actions and behaviour and always resist the temptation to nag and criticise.

One of the things I have noticed about couples who have been married for a long time is that they tend to grow to look similar in some kind of way - strange but true.

The implications of marriage and children.

At some point during your married life the subject of when or whether to have children will arise. Trouble starts when one partner feels ready to have them before the other - maybe one should discuss each other's wishes and desires concerning future offspring before entering into wedlock together. I am convinced that no one should feel pressurised into having a child unless they really want them. Children completely change your lifestyle (they are exceedingly expensive to support) and behaviour, and there is no going back - you must be as sure as you can that this is what you really want before even contemplating having them - for their sakes as well as your own. Although children can enrich your lives and add a new dimension to your relationship, and I for one will never regret the decision to have mine, many couples live very happy and fruitful lives without ever feeling the need to have children.

Having had the children the wife may decide that for financial reasons or her own sanity, she needs to go back to work. Again this needs a lot of discussion between the two of you and a mutual agreement reached in order to avoid disaster.

If you both go out to work you need to share the chores, sometimes one partner feels they are doing more than the other, and it even happens that both feel they are doing more than the other. In order to avoid massive resentments and rows you need to nip this in the bud as soon as possible, and decide who is going to do what.

Above all you need to learn to listen to each other, talk to each other, and constantly re-appraise the situation so that you both grow in the same direction. Often when people don't, they go off at a tangent and grow apart - this path usually leads straight to the marriage guidance counsellors and divorce courts.

I was once told that if you fall *in* love with someone you must eventually fall *out* of love with them. If this is so, then that is the time really to set to work to build up your relationship - this is where all the liking and respect for each other must come to the fore, and the willingness to make the relationship survive.

It is impossible to say, now you are married, that you will never be attracted to anyone else because, like it or not, it will probably happen to one or both of you, especially if you are experiencing difficulties in your relationship. The answer is to look but keep your distance, and always bear in mind the possible consequences if you stray.

All you really need to make a happy and contented marriage is love and respect for each other, and the self determination and constant effort to make it work.

Chapter 8

The Seven Year Itch

Is it really a phenomenon?
Unfortunately, I think it is. What happens is that many people fall in love, get married, and for about two years they are extremely happy with each other. Reality starts to set in, the fairy tale is over, life gets a little mundane and boring, and romance dies. To pep things up they come up with a solution 'Let's have a baby'. Romance re-appears as they start to court each other again to conceive a child, and they experience the expectant feelings of pregnancy. Then there is the excitement of the unknown during pregnancy, and total joy at the birth of their baby. Another two years go by with the fascination of watching the baby develop into an exhausting toddler, and eventually their lives become routinely boring again. 'Let's have another baby' is the solution and another new adventure begins.

The bills start to pile up as life becomes more expensive with two children to support, and one or both of them spends more time away from home trying to make enough money to make ends meet. The first baby reaches school age, the second is now a toddler, and the parents grow complacent with each other, not bothering to make an effort to keep the spark of attraction for each other alive.

Life has fallen into routine habits - they have probably let themselves go physically to pot, and romance is dead. Seven years have gone by, they have ceased to communicate their needs to each other, mutual respect has gone, and they have fallen out of love. If only they had been told before they embarked on their initial adventure of settling down together that all relationships have to be constantly worked at, that love starved of romantic effort will eventually die.

I was once told that love is an itch around the heart that you cannot scratch. The seven year itch tends to attach itself to the mind, and however hard you want to scratch it, it makes your mind wander onto other possibilities in life. Your partner has ceased to be attractive to you, and having lost romantic interest in them your thoughts turn to the possible attractiveness of others. The rot sets in, and one or both of you may start an extra-marital affair, or simply decide to cut your losses and end the marriage.

I have often pondered as to whether or not it would be a good idea for us all to get married on a five year contract. At the end of every five years the marriage would be nullified and we would have to renew our marriage vows. My theory behind this suggestion relates to the way a government is elected. We elect the government for fixed term of years, usually four or five, and at first they work hard to please and impress us all. In the middle of the period they get complacent and the country starts falling apart - however towards the end of this period they wish to get re-elected and make a real effort to get things right again. If the seven year itch phenomenon is to be believed, and that countless marriages crumble after seven years, would it not be better if we all made supreme efforts every five years to put our marriage to rights?

Reasons why marriages break down

Geographic separation for any reason
In this present day climate work is scarce, and we have to take advantage of any work opportunities that present themselves to us. This means that many husbands, and sometimes wives, have to work long distances away from home. The family is already established in one part of the country with the children settled in good schools for them, the spouse has a job which they cannot afford to give up, and so they are split up all week, or maybe weeks on end, whilst the other partner has to work far away from home. Absence, of course, can make the heart grow fonder, but very often distance can lead to estrangement.

Some jobs such as the navy, merchant navy, work on oil rigs, being a pilot or air stewardess, or an international jet-setting career, put particular pressures on a marriage because of the length of time these people need to spend away from home, and of course while the cat's away, the mouse might play.

Very often the business host company will arrange *entertainment* for the visiting business man/woman and this can lead to all kinds of temptations being put in the way. It takes a strong character with a strong relationship to resist such temptations.

Work
One or both partners may get so engrossed in their work, which takes up so much of their time, that they cease to put enough effort into their involvement with the family. Their husband/wife and children may get neglected, leading to resentment, and eventually estrangement.

The working partner mixes with different people at work and may start to develop new interests and friends, joining them socially and excluding their wife/husband. They may fancy someone in this social scene, which can lead to all kinds of complications, and possible estrangement from their partner.

It is important to strike a healthy balance between one's work and personal life. We need to make a positive effort never to let our work overtake our family commitments. Of course it is not an easy thing to do, but what is the point of being successful in your job, only to possibly lose those nearest and dearest to you along the way. It is important also to avoid temptations at work as much as possible by talking enthusiastically about your wife/husband and family (not pretending they don't exist), and taking care to include your spouse in work connected social activities and business trips, as much as possible.

Sport

Golfing widows and *sailing widows* immediately spring to mind here. It is important for us all to indulge in a sport which we enjoy, and even more important to include our partner as much as possible in this activity. If, for example, you are a keen golfer and your partner does not play, then try to encourage them to learn the sport for themselves. If this does not interest them, ask them to accompany you around the course sometimes, to watch you play. If neither of these tactics works, then ask them to join you and your fellow golfers for drinks in the clubhouse when you have finished your game. I cannot stress enough, how important it is to make your partner feel wanted, and not excluded from your activities. If you exclude them, not only will it create resentment but you may find that in spending so much time away from each other, you cultivate a separate circle of friends which could lead to you both drifting apart.

Greater freedom and mobility

The greater freedom and mobility of each partner these days allows more encounters with other potential partners than ever before, and leads to greater temptation. As explained earlier in this book, life in the past was a lot simpler. People rarely travelled far from home because transport was more difficult, and they didn't have so many opportunities to mix with strangers. There were fewer divorces in those days, because women stayed at home more, and did not have the freedom and mobility which they enjoy today. Now that they are liberated and can earn their own living, they are free to go anywhere and do anything they like, which means there is far more chance of meeting temptation.

Growing apart

Many marriages are founded on the dominance of one partner and the submission and dependence of the other. For example, hypothetically, a couple marry in their early twenties and he is a few years older than she. He has a responsible job with a promising career, and his role in the marriage is that of the bread-winner - she is working as a secretary to fill in time before she has children.

After about five years of marriage they are a family with two or three children, and his work is given a lot of importance - he gains a higher status in the family as his money supports them. She supports him, in a more submissive and domestic role, by looking after the home and children, and making life as comfortable as she can for him. His successes become her successes, his crises become her crises, and his social contacts become their friends - her friends are women of a similar ilk, and with whom she can discuss her children, and her husband's triumphs and failures. Both of them are probably acting out the way they have been brought up, by their parents, to believe a marriage should be - he has the role of the dominant bread-winner, she has the role of the submissive wife and mother.

After a few years, she begins to feel trapped, frustrated and dissatisfied, and starts wingeing at her husband. He gets irritated and tells her to stop feeling sorry for herself, do something about her life, be more independent and go out and get a job. She now feels confused, insecure and upset, because she feels that he is pushing her away, wanting her to be different from the submissive domestic girl he married, and she blames herself, just as she has always done when he gets angry, and wonders where she went wrong - she becomes even more clingy.

He is more and more pre-occupied with his work, and is well on his way up the promotional ladder. He has to meet and entertain, and be entertained by many different people, and he begins to change. He becomes more assertive and less tolerant of his wife and his family's weaknesses, and the last thing he wants around his neck, is a wingeing, clinging wife. His life is full of opportunities, and he begins to seek out the company of more exciting women. He has affairs, and although she may also have an affair, she has counselling and therapy.

She gets a greater insight into her character and behaviour, and realises that she has probably spent most of her life being a *doormat*, being dominated at first by her parents and then by her husband. She decides to break her dependency from all of them and take responsibility for her own life. She gets herself a job, makes new friends and begins to stand up to her husband, and assert herself in the home. She demands equality and insists that he shares the workload at home, including the bringing up of the children.

He feels threatened and anxious and begins to fear that he may have created a monster in his life. He argues that she does not need to work, that he is probably paying for her to work by employing nannies and baby-sitters, and that the children will suffer. He may threaten her with divorce, which might well have the desired outcome of bringing her back to heel and into her submissive role again. However, his threats may have no effect at all and their marriage will be in jeopardy.

He may leave her for a younger woman, who will once more be in awe of him, and allow him to have a dominant role. He may, however, revert to the submissive role in the family, out of fear of losing something he depends on, whilst she becomes more dominant. He may whine that she has changed, she is not the girl he married, and may even become a heavy drinker out of self pity and the need to manipulate his wife.

Her career starts to take off and she develops interests outside the home with a new circle of friends, and maybe a lover, and no longer mixes with her old friends or their mutual friends. As long as one of them is still dependent on the other, the fear of divorce will keep them together. However, the dominant partner will not be satisfied, and although the marriage may continue in name, sex and communication has broken down between them, and they lead separate lives.

They have both changed, and instead of growing together, they have grown apart.

There could be a different ending to this story, if both of them love each other enough to re-evaluate their relationship. If both of them work hard to respect the other's need for independence, and if they stop having two separate roles of dominance and dependence. If they start to allow each other the freedom and space to grow as individuals, support and encourage each other, then their marriage will have happy and exciting possibilities.

Wrong choice of partner
Many of us choose the wrong partner in the beginning, because we have extremely low self esteem. We do not choose those who treat us well, and may even despise them, for we have such a low opinion of ourselves that we know we are not worthy of being treated well. We make ourselves into victims, and choose the bastards and bitches who treat us badly,

and in a way we respect them for it, because we know we are not worth any more.

The reason for our low self esteem may go back to our childhood, and stem from an overpowering and dominant father or mother. A lot of people spend years in therapy trying to find out the cause of why they behave in a certain way, and although I think it is interesting to find out why, and it feels good to unburden ourselves to someone else, I feel a lot of time and money is wasted in finding excuses for our behaviour. The ultimate answer lies within us, and we eventually have to get to grips with what has happened in the past and move on. Far too many people blame circumstances, events and people, when the real responsibility for their life lies within them. We can't change others, but we can change ourselves. We need to re-educate ourselves to realise which partners will be good for us and make us happy, and which will just cause us misery. We only have one life - it is not a rehearsal, it is the one and only performance - and we should strive to make it as pleasant and happy as we possibly can, both for ourselves, and for those around us.

Changes in a partner
Many people put on an act to the rest of the world, for whatever reason, and they may hoodwink us into believing they are different from what they really are. After a few years of marriage the mask begins to drop, and displeasing facets of their character emerge, as there

is no need for pretence because they have got what they wanted. If this happens, you need the strength of character to help them to see that unless they make an effort to make that old mask become a reality, they may lose what they have got.

Violence and cruelty

On the other hand, life may not be that simple and your partner may turn out to be a violent and/or cruel person. This can be terrifying, and a lot of courage is needed to seek help and support as soon as possible, to protect you and, if you have any, your children. All too easily you can fall into the battered wife/husband syndrome which is a sickness in itself. If nothing can change your partner back into the person they purported to be at the beginning of your marriage, my advice would be, that you should look after your own and your children's safety, and leave as soon as you possibly can - try to start a new life for yourselves, however financially and emotionally hard it may be.

Alcoholism

Sometimes one partner will change from being a heavy social drinker into an alcoholic, and this is the cause of many failed marriages. Not only is the alcoholic affected, his/her partner gets sick as well. Alcoholism is like a merry-go-round where each participant keeps going round in circles, and has an essential part to play. The alcoholic needs an excuse to drink and their partner unwittingly provides it - for example the wife will start to nag her husband about his drinking, and he will then have an excuse to go off and drink, to get away from her nagging. Every member of the family will eventually ride on this sick merry-go-round, until eventually someone has the courage to get off it. Until the non drinking partner can realise that nothing whatever they could do, can stop their partner drinking, they will be an integral part of the illness.

It is the alcoholic's choice as to whether he/she drinks themselves to death, and until they reach their rock bottom and decide to give it up for themselves, there is absolutely nothing anyone else can do about it. Once they have made the decision to help themselves, help is at hand via Alcoholics Anonymous or *drying out clinics*. Until that time, much help and advice can be given to the non drinking partner and family, via Alcoholics Anonymous Family Group - a marvellous self help group which will help heal them, and enable them to step off the merry-go-round. This will leave the alcoholic without an excuse as to why they should drink to excess, and hopefully give them the opportunity to take responsibility for their own life.

Look in the telephone directory for the number of your local branch of Alcoholics Anonymous.

There may also be an Alcoholics Anonymous Family Group in your area. Again, consult the telephone directory for details.

Drugs

Drug abuse can cause mental and physical changes in anyone, and the misery it brings can hardly be conducive towards a successful and happy marriage.

If you should find that your partner is suffering from a drug problem there are organisations that can help. Try contacting a drugs helpline or a local support group. Your doctor may also be able to help you.

Appearance

Once they have a ring on their finger, some people feel that they have achieved their goal, and there is no need to keep up appearances. They take their partner's feelings for them for granted, and make little or no effort to stay attractive for them. Wives, who have had children, are often at fault here - they put on enormous amounts of weight during pregnancy, and after the birth they get so wrapped up in motherhood, they never make the effort to regain their original shape. They let their figures and general appearance go to pot, and romance flies out of the window as they become more and more *mumsey*. They lose interest in their spouse as a person, and are amazed when their husband deserts them for a more stimulating and exciting woman.

Appearances are important, and we should all work at making ourselves as pleasant to look at as we possibly can, in fairness to our partner. It is not impossible to regain your shape after childbirth, as many of us have proved, it just takes a lot of determination and hard work. It is stupid to take your partner's feelings for granted, by ignoring their needs and not bothering to keep up appearances, for you may be taking the risk of losing their affections for you. Make time for your husband as well as for your children, and make the effort to do some exercise - maybe join a gym, take up a sport, join *Weight Watchers* - and develop healthy eating patterns. If you have children you will be setting a good and useful example, which will hopefully benefit them in years to come. Any relationship involves hard work and effort but it pays off in the end.

Money
Although money can't buy you happiness, it can certainly help to make life more comfortable, and the lack of it can sometimes destroy a marriage.

When young people get married, they often have a simple and idealistic view that money can't buy you happiness, and love is all you need for a happy and successful marriage.

At the beginning of their marriage, this is probably true, and although they do not have much money, just being together makes them blissfully happy. A few years later though, they have a couple of children and they need a larger home. Only one of them is the bread-winner now, whilst the other stays at home to take care of the children. As the children become more demanding and expensive, the bills pile up, money is scarce, and pressure is put on the breadwinner to go out and make some more. The parents are tired and fraught with financial worries, resentments build up and life is no longer a carefree and happy existence. As the tension builds up, the arguments begin, romantic love takes a back seat, and the marriage is in jeopardy.

There is a saying, *Marry in haste, repent at leisure.* Make sure, before you marry, that you understand all the implications that marriage will bring, financial as well as emotional. Work hard together to improve your finances, and don't contemplate having children until you think you can afford to support them. If your marriage should fall on hard times, try to pull through together and never apportion the blame for your financial problems onto either party. If you need it, seek professional help from your bank and/or accountant, and listen to their advice. There are few people who travel through life without incurring some kind of financial difficulties - the clever ones will find a way round them. *Where there is a will, there is a way.*

Infidelity

Whatever the causes are for one partner being unfaithful to the other, infidelity is a real testing time in any relationship. Although surveys show that people are becoming more forgiving of infidelity, and that fewer relationships break up because of it, adultery is a dangerous course to take if you place any value on your marriage.

Should you be the one to stray, you have two choices. The first is to say nothing, in order to cause as little hurt to your partner as possible, and hope that they will never find out. If you do this, you must also be fully aware that the consequences, should they find out for themselves, will be far greater than if you had told them yourself to start with. Or you can choose to be open and honest with your partner; say how sorry you are, that this has never happened before (and I hope it hasn't!) and that you will make sure that it never happens again. You will be bound to go through a rocky patch, but I think you may find that honesty is the best policy - if your partner truly loves you they will eventually forgive you.

It is essential, if you feel there is something lacking in your relationship, to make as much effort as you can to work it out, rather than going for the easy option of seeking solace elsewhere.

If you are the partner who has been cheated on, try to view your marriage as a whole, not just this one incident, before coming to any decision. Remember that it is not events that upset us, it is the way we react to them. Jealousy and mistrust may be particular problems that have to be overcome following infidelity, and the way in which these emotions are handled are vital in securing the relationship.

Children

When we get married it is expected that we will eventually produce children, but for some couples this is not necessarily the right course of action for them. Having a child will change your life, both emotionally and financially, and unless both of you really want a child it is better to delay the decision, or decide not to have children at all. Some people find they can't cope with being a parent, can't come to terms with the inevitable changes in their partner and with having to share their partner's affections with the child, and the marriage may fall apart. There are enough new babies being born each day, and many childless couples live very happy lives together, sometimes taking pleasure in looking after other people's children, and also in the fact that they can escape from them at any time.

However, some marriages break up because of the lack of children. It is always better to discuss the issue of whether or not you want to have children, before you get married - if one marriage partner desperately wants a child and the other does not, resentments will build up whether they eventually have a child or not, and the partnership will often break up. Some people, for whatever medical reason, find they cannot have a child, and although they may be able to adopt one, this is sometimes not acceptable to one of the partners, and it may cause the marriage to end.

Therefore I must stress again, that to start a marriage without having previously discussed each other's views on having children, is sheer folly. It is essential to make sure before you marry, that you both want the same goals in life, in order to avoid the problems already mentioned. Of course neither of you will know before you try, if either or both of you are unable to reproduce. If this situation occurs, you will need to draw on all your tolerance, care and understanding for your partner. Hopefully you will have discussed each other's views on adoption before getting married, and if adoption is not for you, there is, fortunately these days, much medical help at hand, which may enable you to conceive the child that you both long for.

Illness
A sudden major and ongoing illness in one partner will put pressure on any marriage, however good the relationship may be, and sometimes the worry and strain on the other will prove to be too much for them.

Try to think positively, and treasure each moment you have together. Try to make the illness draw you closer together in your fight against it, and accept as much help as you can from friends and organisations who will assist in taking the pressure off you. Be as tolerant and understanding as you can, whether you are the one struck by illness, or the carer. By always trying look on the bright side, you can both help each other through this painful and difficult period of life together.

Retirement

Some men spend their lives planning and saving for the day they will eventually be able to retire from work, and in so doing they may waste, and cease to enjoy, many precious present moments. What they may not have taken into account, in their excited anticipation, is the strain that retirement could put on their marriage. Often the wife will have built up an independent life at home, and may find it difficult to cope with having a husband around all the time. Being permanently together may throw up cracks in their relationship that they had not realised before, inflation may cause economic hardship, and they may also run out of conversation. How many times have we all sat in a restaurant and observed an older married couple sitting opposite each other and not saying a word? Most people will have enough feelings for each other to come to terms with the situation, but it is becoming increasingly common for such marriages to fail.

It is therefore essential to have discussions with your partner, well in advance of the proposed retirement date, about every potential problem that could occur, and to try to work out solutions to them in case they should ever arise. It is wise for you both not only to pay into a pension plan at as young an age as possible, but also to make sure it is, if possible, inflation linked with a reputable company. It is also extremely important to cultivate hobbies and interests of your own before retirement, so that you can maintain a degree of independence afterwards. It is equally important to cultivate joint interests and hobbies that you can share together - if you can achieve both separate and joint activities, you will have plenty to talk about. Retirement is an ideal period of life to visit places and people you have rarely had the time and opportunity to visit before. If you can respect each other's space, as well as giving each other the support and companionship you both need, retirement should not present too many problems for you.

Help from friends, marriage guidance services and charities
When we have problems in our personal lives, I think we all have difficulty in sorting them out on our own. In the end it is down to us, ourselves, to make the final decisions, but it certainly helps to have others to whom we can unburden our troubles. Real friends are especially important in times of need as they know us well, and are probably familiar with those connected with our dilemma. Not only will it help us to use them as a sounding board, but they will hopefully be able to give us constructive criticism and advice as well.

If you feel you need further professional advice to help sort out your marriage difficulties, there are well known organisations to contact, such as Relate, as well as individual professional counsellors. You will find them in the telephone directory.

If you ring them, they will put you in touch with professionally trained counsellors who are skilled in helping with all matters concerning relationship difficulties. They will listen to you, and help you to decide what is the best course of action for you, and if necessary, (if both you and your partner are willing) they will counsel you both together. If you eventually decide that the best solution would be for you and your partner to separate, they will help you to do so as painlessly as possible for all concerned.

Should you at any time feel absolutely desperate or suicidal because of the breakdown of your marriage, help is always at hand, 24 hours a day, via The Samaritans - just phone the telephone operator to be put through.

If you feel you would like to contact local organisations for particular needs, telephone your local Citizens' Advice Bureau for all the contact telephone numbers and addresses in your area. Also do not forget that your local doctor and clergyman may also be able to help you with many difficulties that may arise.

You are not alone, there is always someone out there who will help and advise.

Ending the relationship
If you are absolutely sure that you no longer wish to continue with your marriage, and have carefully considered all the possible consequences, there are

various options open to you. You can try for a decree of nullity, a decree of judicial separation, or divorce.

Nullity

A decree of nullity will end a marriage in a similar way to a decree of divorce, when it is proved that the marriage was never valid from the beginning - it is null and void. The grounds for nullity are:

Bigamy

If one partner was already married at the time of the wedding ceremony, the marriage is void.

Age

If one partner was under the age of sixteen at the time of the wedding ceremony, the marriage is void.

Relationship

In this country you cannot marry your parent, grandparent, child, brother/sister, niece/nephew, aunt/uncle, step relations (relations of half blood) and illegitimate children relatives, and certain relations by marriage e.g. your daughter's widower. If you do, the marriage is void.

Defects in formalities

Some formal defects such as the banns not being properly called, or the licence not being properly obtained may make the marriage void.

Non consummation

If the marriage has never been consummated because one partner is incapable of having sexual intercourse, or one partner refuses ever to have sex, the marriage is void.

Lack of consent

If one partner consented to marry the other through fear, duress or insanity at the time of the wedding ceremony, the marriage is void.

Mental disorder

If one partner is proved to have been mentally unfit for marriage at the time of the wedding ceremony, the marriage is void.

Venereal disease

If one partner was suffering from a communicable form of venereal disease at the time of the wedding ceremony, and the other partner was unaware of this, the marriage can be declared void.

Pregnancy by another

If the wife was pregnant by someone other than the husband at the time of the wedding ceremony, and the husband was unaware of this fact, the marriage can be declared void.

With reference to the grounds of lack of consent, mental disorder, venereal disease and pregnancy by another, there may be time limits during which proceedings must begin. The above information is intended only as general guidelines: laws vary from country to country and from state to state, so check the legal position where you live to see what your rights are. The same applies to the information on divorce given below.

Judicial separation

If you do not wish, for religious or financial reasons, to end the marriage by divorce, you can petition for a decree of judicial separation at any time after the marriage. This will not end the marriage and neither partner is free to remarry. It gives the court's seal of approval to you both living apart and, as in a divorce, the court will resolve the problems concerned with the separation, such as finances, property and children. The procedure for obtaining this decree is almost the same that for obtaining a divorce, except there is one decree for judicial separation and two for divorce - the preliminary decree nisi and the decree absolute.

Divorce

Divorce is very final, and should not be used as a threatening device to get your partner back - it will not work. Be absolutely sure as to your motives in wanting this divorce, and be absolutely sure that this is the path that you wish to follow.

Legal requirements for divorce

There are certain legal requirements that must be satisfied before you can be granted a divorce. These vary between countries so check the position where you live. As a general rule, however, divorces are not available during the first year of marriage.

Irretrievable breakdown of the marriage

The only basic ground for divorce is that the marriage has broken down irretrievably. The court is not concerned with apportioning blame to either party, it just has to be satisfied that the marriage is finally over, and that there is no chance of the partners getting back together again. Breakdown can be proved only if one of five *facts* can be established by the petitioning partner. The five *facts* are:

1. Adultery

Adultery is sexual intercourse with someone of the opposite sex, other than your spouse. A divorce can be granted if the petitioner can prove that the respondent has committed adultery, and that the petitioner finds it intolerable to live with the respondent.

2. Behaviour

The petitioner has to show the court that the respondent has behaved in such an unacceptable way, that they cannot reasonably be expected to live with him/her any more - *unreasonable behaviour*.

Examples of unreasonable behaviour could be: violence, regular drunkenness, drug addiction, excessive sexual demands or sexual perversions, no sex at all, persistent abuse, neglect, homosexual conduct, criminal tendencies, placing unreasonable restrictions on the personal freedom of the petitioner, mental or physical illness which creates intolerable demands on the petitioner, etc.

3. Desertion
The petitioner must prove that the respondent has deserted the home, or driven the petitioner out of the home by his/her conduct against the petitioner's will, for a continuous period of at least two years immediately before the presentation of the divorce petition.

4. Separation for two years
If you have lived continuously apart for two years immediately before the presentation of the petition, and the respondent consents at the time they are notified of the filing of the petition and, consents at the time the decree nisi is pronounced, the divorce can be granted.

5. Separation for five years
A petition can be filed if you both have lived apart for a continuous period of at least five years immediately prior to the presentation of the petition, even if the respondent does not consent to it.

Effect on the children
No child likes change, and any child will find it difficult to accept that the family life they were used to has

now gone for good. However, if the marriage has completely broken down, they will usually suffer less distress in the long run having their parents living apart, than if they had stayed in a home full of friction with both parents.

It is possibly a good idea, at the start of the proceedings, to sit down with your children and explain to them exactly what is going to happen, and what your plans are. They need to know as soon as possible where they are to live and with whom; how often and when they will be with the parent they are not living with; that finances will not be as plentiful as before, because there will be two homes to support or buy. It is better that they know the facts from the beginning so that nothing comes as a surprise to them, and this also means that they will have maximum time to adjust to the new situation.

A lot of patience will be needed to combat problems such as the children not being able to forgive the parent who leaves, and also the cruel remarks that are very often said by the child to the parent they live with - the child is hurting inside, and this sometimes makes him/her want to hurt their nearest and dearest.

Everyone reacts differently to stress, and you both have to make a real effort to make the divorce as painless as possible for the children, with as little disruption as possible. Children need a stable background, and they could have problems in their future marriage if they do not have some stability that they can relate to.

It is important that you back each other up at all times with reference to the children, and that neither of you attempts to make the children take sides against the other parent. One parent may find, or may have found, a new partner who does not treat the children well, and who may also resent the time and money spent on the children. If this happens, you must give serious consideration as to whether the right choice of partner has been made - your children must always come first. If you find you have serious difficulties with the children, seek help as soon as possible from those qualified to deal with such problems - you could discuss the matter with your doctor and the children's teachers. It is a good idea, anyway, to keep in constant contact with the school to find out if there are any signs there, of disturbance over the divorce. Give your children lots of love, support, understanding and security at all times to get them through this difficult period, however bad you may be feeling yourself.

If necessary, there are a number of organisations to contact. Look in your telephone directory for the number of a local branch of one of the following: National Council for One-Parent Families, Gingerbread, Families need Fathers, Rights of Women, Child Poverty Action Group, Family Rights Group. Other local groups may exist in your area.

Chapter 9

Starting Again

Coping with divorce

Divorce is a very frightening word and prospect to those who have not been through the experience; however like everything else in life, reality is far easier to cope with than the fear leading up to it. For most people it is not a pleasant period of life, but like the dreaded visit to the dentist, it is something to endure at the time with the prospect of a more comfortable and happy situation later. Yes I am happy to tell you, many years after my marriage break-up, that there is life after divorce, and a happy and more enlightened one for most.

As with the breakdown of any relationship, one of the main things to realise is that the situation is not unique to you alone - that others are not seeing you as a failure (although inside that is naturally how you may see yourself for a while), are not blaming you, and that others want to give you as much support and comfort as they can.

First of all you need to go through a grieving period, and here it is important to remember that it is not only the rejected partner who will suffer - the partner who ends the relationship not only suffers grief, but enormous guilt as well. Now is the time to feel sorry for yourself and to cry - tears were invented for a purpose - make use of them and mentally wash your sorrows away. Men, because of social conditioning, usually find it more difficult to cry than women but it is important that they give equal vent to their feelings. Pour your heart out to your friends, indulge yourself in discussing the situation at length until there is really nothing new to say, and openly accept their support and friendship. However, you must have a mental cut off point! There has to be a deadline when you say to yourself 'I accept that this relationship is over, and I am now going to get on with the rest of my life.' There is a danger, if you don't, of getting addicted to your unhappiness, and also the indulgence of subjecting your friends to your tales of woe. Believe me, if this happens, you will not have too many friends left to bore.

Now is the time to *Pick yourself up, dust yourself down, and start all over again.* Whatever has happened is in the past, and no amount of self recriminations and regrets can change it. These feelings can only waste the most important moment of your life, which is now, and which one day may be your last. So whatever you are doing at any given time, even if you are just washing up the dishes, when painful thoughts from the past start creeping into your mind, deliberately block them out by thinking and concentrating on what you are doing or to whom you are talking at that moment. If you can try to learn from past mistakes, and use the knowledge to good effect in the future, then they will have all been worthwhile. Worrying about what is going to happen to you also wastes your precious present moment. Worry, like regret, is a useless exercise, and unless you make a conscious effort to stop, you will never enjoy any of your present moments. By the time you reach the stage you have been worrying about, you will be on to worrying about something else!

Strangely enough, once your friends and relations feel you are coping, they will feel more comfortable with you and rally round even more. From now on whatever you do or say, do it with dignity. Never make abusive or derogatory remarks about your partner to anyone - leave that to your lawyer if you are using one. This brings me to another point, the legal profession. Some couples are fortunate in the fact that they have an amicable divorce and do not feel the need to employ legal services. However most of us are not so lucky, and it is extremely important to be careful that all the family finances are not frittered away on legal fees, which do not enhance either parties finances, only your lawyer's. Try as much as you can to communicate with your partner and work things out between the two of you. Try not to fall into the trap of treating your lawyer like a counsellor and phoning him/her up at every available opportunity to discuss your latest difficulty. Remember every minute of each telephone call is costing you a lot of money. Also never instruct your lawyer to do anything without first finding out how much it will cost!

There will always be a tendency for the one left behind to feel desperate to dive into a new relationship, maybe to prove to the rest of the world that he/she is still desirable and attractive - please don't! Just because one particular person out of all the thousands of potential partners in the world no longer desires to be with you, is no reason to be desperate. This is the start of a new episode in your life and should be viewed as one more exciting challenge to be overcome. You are just as desirable and attractive as you were before things started to go wrong; you have just had a tremendous blow to your self esteem and confidence, and need time now to build them up before you consider entering in to a new relationship.

Start working on yourself - maybe consider changing your hairstyle and image. This can work wonders in restoring your self confidence. If you can afford it, it is an excellent idea to employ the services of an image and colour co-ordinator consultant to help you launch the *new look* you on to the world. Again if you can afford it, a visit to a health farm for even just a few days, can help make you feel a million dollars again. Making sure you get lots of exercise is an absolute must - this can give you tremendous highs as well as many hours of thought blocking. Why not learn a new sport, start a new hobby, visit the theatre, cinema, museums? Give yourself plenty of new things to do and think about, and also try to read more, especially the newspapers, so that when you do eventually meet someone you would like to spend more time with, you will have plenty of interesting topics to talk about.

It is only when you feel at peace with yourself and are happy in your own company, that you should consider letting someone else enter into your life, and you'll find that is the time when others start being attracted to you. Everyone has problems of their own and the last thing they want to do is to add someone else's problems to their own. A happy, independent and together person is an extremely attractive one.

Coping with any other break of relationship

Loss of a friend

Losing a friend can be devastating, and sometimes more traumatic than breaking up with a partner. There are many reasons why friends break up, and one obvious one that comes to mind would be the friend who runs of with their friend's spouse. However I was once told that there are only two things that people might disagree over and then break up their friendship - children and money. We all get annoyed with our children from time to time, but deep down we are fiercely protective of them, and any friend who actively tries to harm them, by deed or criticism, would find their friendship days with us were numbered. Also, as I have mentioned previously in this book, *never a borrower nor a lender be*. If you can't afford to give your friend the money they would like as a loan, then don't lend it if you value your friendship. In the same way don't ask a friend to loan you money unless you know with absolute certainty, that you can pay it back. The lender will get angry and hurt if they are not paid back, and avoid seeing their friend out of embarrassment because they feel they cannot ask for the loan to be repaid. The borrower will be equally embarrassed that they can't repay the loan; they will avoid the lender and eventually resent the fact that they are in debt to their friend, and even grow to dislike them.

Losing a friend is losing someone to whom you have bared your soul, and placed your absolute trust in. It is the loss of a confidante with whom you could have a laugh and a moan, and someone you could lean on for support in troubled times. You will also experience extreme loneliness.

Again you will need time to grieve and collect your thoughts. You will need to recognise what went wrong in your friendship, and try to learn from the mistakes. Time is a great healer and you will make other friends - you just have to get out there and start making an effort all over again. The world is full of lonely people who would be delighted to be your friend, once you have made the effort to approach them and proffer your friendship.

Relationships at work
Unless you are an employer yourself, not many people realise how upsetting and disruptive it can be to lose an employee that you felt was indispensable. An employer will put their trust in the loyalty of an employee, and it can be traumatic if they find that their employee has betrayed their trust, and maybe disclosed confidential information to a rival company. An employee that suddenly walks out and leaves the employer in the lurch because they have found more lucrative employment, is also a tremendous loss. It is equally disturbing if the employer realises that it was their fault that their employee left. For example working in a close environment and coping with the stress and pressure of the job, can magnify even fairly minor problems such as the employee who is constantly late for work, or who is habitually untidy, or who eats all the office biscuits and doesn't replace them. The silliest of things get out of perspective, and the employer explodes into anger resulting in the employee walking out.

Luckily for employers the work situation nowadays is so grim, that it is fairly easy to find new employees. At the same time it is still a disruption that no busy office really needs, and the employer would be well advised to be more careful next time in their choice of employee, and if the fault was theirs, to think long and hard about their own attitudes in the working environment.

The loss of your job and employer can be pretty devastating too, not only because of the loss of livelihood and the worry and uncertainty that brings, but also the loss of comradeship of your fellow workers. Unfortunately it happens all the time, sometimes through no fault of our own, if the company is in financial difficulties, and we just have gather our wits about us, regain our confidence and set out in search of new employment. Again a lot of soul searching is needed to ascertain whether or not it was our fault that we lost our employment. If we were in the wrong, then having come to terms with the facts, we are in an excellent position to learn from past mistakes, and forge ahead to a brighter future.

Bereavement
The death of anyone with whom you have had a close relationship, whether it was your father, mother, wife/husband, child or friend brings indescribable grief, sorrow, emptiness, and maybe loneliness. It invariably brings guilt as you regret not having said or done, or having said or done, various things. You blame yourself for actions and words that may have hurt your loved one, and there is a sense of desperation inside you as you realise that it is just too late to do anything about it. The death of a parent also brings fear of our own mortality, as we realise that we are now on the front line.

Time is obviously a great healer, and hopefully we all come to terms with the loss of our dear ones, and although we will never forget them, and indeed we should not, we get on with the general job of living. For some though, it is not that simple. Many bereaved people do not undergo the *right* kind of grieving period at the start. They feel unable to give vent to their feelings to their friends and relations, and maybe rush here, there and everywhere, bottling up their grief, anger and guilt, inside them. This could go on for many years, even for the rest of their lives, and leave them so emotionally damaged that every aspect of their life and relationships will be affected. Such people desperately need help in order to be able to lead happy and fulfilled lives once more, and we all have a responsibility to recognise what is happening to them, and forcibly point them in the direction of professional people who are trained to help in such matters. Only by facing the real truth of any situation and working our grief through it, can any of us in such circumstances start to live again.

The death of a loved pet, can be as painful as the loss of a loved person, especially to children. A pet such as dog, is a friend and companion, and possibly the only living being that gives us totally unconditional love. I don't think many people realise how much support and comfort bereaved pet owners need, and sometimes it's best that they are encouraged to find a replacement as soon as possible. The relationship between a pet and its owner is a special one, and should never be dismissed as being trivial.

How and when to go about looking for a replacement/substitute relationship, if wanted.

When you feel ready, start thinking about ways to meet new friends. If you have taken up a sport and joined a club, that is obviously an excellent way to get started. Also, always try to cultivate new friends of your own sex - everyone has friends of the opposite sex to whom they wish they were attracted but aren't, and they will be at pains to introduce you to them - who knows, one of them might be just right for you!

You could join a dating agency to find yourself a partner. This method does not suit everyone as it can be traumatic to meet a complete stranger on your own, with the added difficulty of extricating yourself from the meeting if you find you don't get on! Also if the person you meet is attracted to you and you are not attracted to them, you could be pestered with unwanted calls. I personally feel it is doubtful that an agency can promise to introduce you to a future husband/wife - there is always the hidden X Factor that no one can predict. In my experience, when someone has told me that they would like to meet a 'tall slim Doctor', they invariably walk off with a 'short fat balding lawyer'.

You could try advertising in one of the many lonely hearts columns in various magazines and newspapers, but as we have all read and heard about in the news, this can be an exceedingly dangerous exercise.

You could go with a friend to a wine bar, pub or even a night-club to meet new people. Again you have to be aware of the dangers of being approached by a married man/woman, and all the heart-aches that go with this when finally you find out, having just lost your heart to him/her. Also, always be aware of the dangers of going out with a complete stranger, whom none of your friends or acquaintances knows anything about.

You could also consider joining an organisation that organises dinner parties, social events and activities for large groups of single people. This decision has the advantage of being a more natural way of making new friends of both sexes. You have the security of knowing that, providing the organisation is a reputable one, all the guests are single, and they are there because they also want to widen their circle of friends. So long as no one has your details, unless you decide to give them out yourself or you have given permission for the organisation to do so, it is a safe way of meeting strangers - there is safety in numbers. This way of meeting new friends can be a marvellous stepping stone back into society as a single person rather than one half of your previous partnership. You must again be careful however, as there is no independent controlling body over these organisations, to check the company's credentials. Make sure that they have a proven track record, that they have been running for at least two years, and that they have plenty of members of the opposite sex to introduce you to!

However you decide to find a new relationship, bear in mind that discussing your divorce and emotional problems should be taboo! Just be a happy, fun, relaxed person that others would like to be with, and you'll find you are spoilt for choice.

In what way are things different the second time around?

Hopefully the second time around you will have thought long and hard about the mistakes you have made in the past, you will have learnt some useful knowledge and be somewhat wiser. Hopefully you will have more idea as to the kind of person with whom you feel you will be happy, and can have a more balanced relationship. I do advise you, though, not to be too specific in your requirements. I know a lot of single people have checklists as to the exact type they would like to meet, and if their new potential partner falls short of any of these, they quickly move on to the next. As I have said many times before in this book, no one is perfect, and if you are continually searching for perfection you may land up being single, permanently. Please throw away those checklists! Try to be more flexible, and remember it is impossible to change someone else, (unless they want to change themselves), but it is always possible to change yourself. Maybe if your relationships repeatedly go wrong, that is what is needed.

Do people make the same mistakes, or are they wiser the second time around?
Many people continually go for the same type and end up being hurt. Sometimes it could be that subconsciously we are recreating a dominant father/mother figure in our partners, and indeed this same pattern might have been repeated throughout whole generations of our families. If you suspect that this could be the case with you, I do urge you seek to some counselling advice. It is amazing how breaking these patterns can very often lead to true and lasting happiness. You just need the courage to recognise it.

Hopefully the second time around you will have learnt that nothing in this life is a certainty - just when you think your life is running smoothly, and that you have everything under control, life has a funny way of switching things round and proving you wrong. This happens to everyone and is just another one of life's hurdles to be overcome, and each time you come out the victor, you are that much stronger in yourself. If you can always bear in mind that each relationship has to be constantly worked at, even when you are feeling blissfully happy within it, that life is a succession of changes including the way we ourselves change, and can frequently re-evaluate your relationship together, you will have more than a fighting chance of success. Never take anyone or anything for granted; communicate, negotiate, compromise, think positively, concentrate on the good points and stop nit-picking at the bad; give your partner space, trust, and understanding; see humour in the direst of situations and laugh; love and appreciate yourself, banish fear of the unknown, and make an effort to keep the romance alive.

One of my favourite songs is by Sammy Cahn and it begins *Love is lovelier the second time around, just as wonderful with both feet on the ground,* and to my mind this says it all. If you are wise and can learn from past mistakes, keeping level-headed at the same time as falling in love, these words could indeed be true for you.

Epilogue

By Matt Mountebank
Author of How To Chat-up Women

Relationships are the toughest things on earth to get to grips with, understand and control. It can take a lifetime of being battered by rejection, loneliness and break-ups before the puzzle finally makes sense, before all the pieces fit, and before you know precisely how you fit into the whole thing yourself.

To all those *lost jig-saw pieces* out there, who may be lacking optimism that all will eventually come right, I would like to quote some wise words penned by John Lennon in *Beautiful Boy*,

Life is what happens to you
While you're busy making other plans.

No matter how hard we try to shape our own destinies, random events are thrown at us daily, overturning, negating or accelerating the plans we have made. Call it fate, chance, coincidence or luck, the point is that none of us has complete control over our relationships because we cannot control the interactions and experiences of others around us. By doing *the right thing* (as outlined in this book) wherever possible in order to develop and maintain our relationships we are giving ourselves the best possible chance of success. But success (or failure) cannot be conjured up by simply mixing the right recipe. A chance happening can change things overnight, for better or for worse, and your life can take a completely different direction.

That chance factor is what makes life so challenging. If you rise to the challenge and thrive on changes, improvements and adaptation, your life will be all the more rewarding. Relationships take you on a complex and twisting road, through unseen hazards and unimagined opportunities, but with a guide like Hillie Marshall you will be able to cope with it.

If you are thinking, 'But my life won't change, I'll always be doing this same routine', look back 10 or 15 years, and ask yourself if you could ever have imagined being where you are today? The changes in life are not always dramatic: they can be slow and subtle, but you can see how far you have come when you look at it over a number of years.

Accept change, accept the influence of random events, and then steer a course through all that life throws at you with the help of *Hillie Marshall's Guide To Successful Relationships*.

Bibliography

(And recommended further reading)

Men Are From Mars, Women Are From Venus
John Gray Ph.D.   *Harper Collins*

Your Erroneous Zones
Dr. Wayne W. Dyer   *Warner Books*

How To Chat-up Women
Matt Mountebank   *Summersdale*

The Divorce Handbook
Jenny Levin   *Sphere*

Divorce -
The Things You Thought You'd Never Need To Know
J. M. Black   *Right Way*

Wedding Etiquette
Pat & Bill Derraugh   *Foulsham*